P9-CFI-043

Using Computers to Teach Literature

NCTE Editorial Board: Jacqueline Bryant, Kermit Campbell, Bobbi Fisher, Xin Liu Gale, Sarah Hudelson, Bill McBride, Gerald R. Oglan, Helen Poole, Karen Smith, Chair, ex officio, Pete Feely, ex officio

GRACE LIBRARY CARLOW COLLEGE
PITTSBURGH PA 15213

Using Computers to Teach Literature

A Teacher's Guide

LB
1050.37
J63
1998

SECOND EDITION OF

Computer Conversations
Readers and Books Online

Marilyn Jody
Western Carolina University

Marianne Saccardi
Norwalk Community-Technical College

National Council of Teachers of English
1111 W. Kenyon Road, Urbana, Illinois 61801-1096

CATALOGUED

Prepress Services: Precision Graphics

Staff Editor: Zarina Hock

Cover Design: Precision Graphics

Interior Design: Mary C. Cronin

Cover Photography: © Elizabeth Crews

NCTE Stock Number: 08253-3050

© 1998 by the National Council of Teachers of English. All rights reserved. Printed in the United States of America.

It is the policy of NCTE in its journals and other publications to provide a forum for the open discussion of ideas concerning the content and the teaching of English and the language arts. Publicity accorded to any particular point of view does not imply endorsement by the Executive Committee, the Board of Directors, or the membership at large, except in announcements of policy, where such endorsement is clearly specified.

Library of Congress Cataloging-in-Publication Data
Jody, Marilyn, 1932-
 Using computers to teach literature : a teacher's guide / Marilyn Jody, Marianne Saccardi.
  p. cm.
 Rev. ed. of : Computer conversations. c1996.
 Includes bibliographical references (p.).
 ISBN 0-8141-0825-3
 1. Reading--Computer-assisted instruction. 2. Language arts--Computer-assisted instruction. 3. Children--United States--Books and reading. 4. World Wide Web (Information retrieval system)
I. Saccardi, Marianne. II. Jody, Marilyn, 1932- Computer conversations. III. Title.
 LB1050.37.J63 1998
 428.4'0285--dc21   98-47500
                                                       CIP

CATALOGUED

To our students, who continue to inspire us, and to teachers everywhere who have accepted the challenge of education in our time.

To those whose love and support make all things possible— my family and my extended family—Joanne, Jack, and Christy.—MJ

To my husband, Thomas, and my sons, Christopher and Daniel, who have taught me everything I know about computers.—MS

Contents

Acknowledgments

We will be forever grateful to Patti Johnson and Bonnie Beam at WCU MicroNet, whose patience and good will are beyond measure. Without their knowledge of computers and networks, both of us would still be writing with quill pens, and BookRead would be only a dream.

We are indebted to those wonderfully courageous authors who ventured into the classrooms of cyberspace with us: Sue Ellen Bridgers, Cynthia DeFelice, Jean Craighead George, Gary Paulsen, and Ann Turner.

And we owe our thanks to those students, teachers, media specialists, and school administrators who gave so generously of their precious time in order to create computer conversations about books. The following schools, teachers, and staff deserve our special appreciation for their pioneering participation in our early BookRead Projects and workshops:

Andrews High School, Andrews, North Carolina: Carolyn Franks, teacher;

Asheville City Schools, Asheville, North Carolina: June McCracken, computer coordinator;

Asheville High School, Asheville, North Carolina: Diane Rutledge, teacher, and Sylvia Ready, media specialist;

Asheville Middle School, Asheville, North Carolina: Nancy Buchanan, sixth-grade teacher;

Bethel Middle Schools, Waynesville, North Carolina: Tracy Christopher, teacher, and Janice Freeman, computer specialist;

Bruce Drysdale Elementary School, Hendersonville, North Carolina: Paddy Lynch, third-grade teacher;

Canton Middle School, Canton, North Carolina: Nita Matzen, computer specialist;

East Elementary School, Bryson City, North Carolina: Debra Adams, media specialist;

Hendersonville Junior High School, Hendersonville, North Carolina: Nita Matzen, media specialist;

Leadmine Elementary School, Raleigh, North Carolina: Robin Hutchins, teacher, Linda Shearin, media specialist, and Mike Jordan, principal;

Macon Middle School, Franklin, North Carolina: Sherry Henderson, teacher;

Martins Creek School, Murphy, North Carolina: Clara Gustason, fourth-grade teacher, Muffy Kerber, seventh-grade/eighth-grade teacher, and Pat Tagliarini, second-grade teacher;

Nantahala School, Topton, North Carolina: Leslie Orr, teacher, and Judy Morgan, computer specialist;

North Buncombe High School, Weaverville, North Carolina: Melody Eury and Patricia Stevens, teachers;

Port Chester Middle School, Port Chester, New York: Mike DeVito, seventh-grade teacher, and Lucia Langworth and Mary Maguire, media specialists;

Rosman High School, Rosman, North Carolina: Susan Bir, teacher;

Scarsdale High School, Scarsdale, New York: Christopher Renino, teacher;

Smoky Mountain High School, Sylva, North Carolina: Alice Pendergast, teacher;

Tuscola High School, Waynesville, North Carolina: Joyce Lackey and Bonnie Stamey, teachers;

Whitby American Montessori Center, Greenwich, Connecticut: Gerry Leonard and John Gibson, junior high teachers, Deirdre Fennessy, upper-elementary teacher, and Bob Jackson, computer expert.

Finally, we are grateful to our very talented consultants: JoAnn Curtis, Durham, New Hampshire; Margaret Gayle, Raleigh, North Carolina; Kathy Harwood, Statesboro, Georgia; Libby Hodan, Asheville, North Carolina; Nita Matzen, Clyde, North Carolina; and Gail Pitts, Asheville, North Carolina.

Preface to the Revised Edition

When we wrote *Computer Conversations,* we gave the World Wide Web about the same relative amount of space it occupied on the Internet at the time—about a paragraph. Now, only three years later, the Web is widely known as the largest single element on the Net. To no one's real surprise, the ease of using the Web has opened up the Internet to a world that had been waiting for just such a breakthrough. Consequently, even though *Computer Conversations* has only been on the shelves a short time, we decided a revised edition was needed. We have added Chapter 7, "An Introduction to the World Wide Web," in which we describe what "the Web" is; discuss how to gain access to it; how to use "browsers" and "search engines"; list useful sites for English teachers; and suggest ways to use the Web in the language arts curriculum. We hope we have provided the kind of information and impetus you need to begin exploring the World Wide Web with an eye to finding ways to use it for the enrichment of student learning.

In this edition, we have also added a section to Chapter 3 called "Teachable Moments." In the online projects we have coordinated since the book was first written, we have begun to concentrate more closely on what students are saying to each other about books in their computer conversations as a clue to what they need to know to become better readers and writers. In "Teachable Moments" we give examples of how to use what students say about the books they read as a basis for language arts instruction.

As you look through the book, you will note that we have also updated the material to reflect new children's books, the latest electronic texts, new funding sources and staff development opportunities, new developments in state certification requirements, more current resources for teachers, and new directions for computer use in the classroom. Of course, like the world of computers, the uses of technology in the classroom will continue to evolve. We invite you to share your new discoveries with us and with each other as you make telecommunications an integral part of your teaching.

Introduction

This book may be your first venture into computer territory or just one of the many travel guides you have read along the way. In either case, read on. What we do here is to describe our experiences and those of others—beginners, as we all are—in a technology that changes almost daily. We talk about what we have learned in the process and, on that basis, provide what we believe is the kind of information English teachers must have in order to make significant use of these powerful new instructional strategies.

What will the "telecommunications revolution" mean for books and readers as computers enter more and more into the literature classroom? As teachers of literature, we too asked that question, meanwhile coping with word-processing programs, electronic games, and classrooms where children were more "hooked" on Nintendo™ than on books. Then words like "e-mail" and "Internet" appeared. Suddenly, it seemed like everyone was talking about an "information highway," yet no one we knew seemed clear about where it was going to take us. We wanted to know what "telecommunications" had to do with us as teachers. We wanted to know whether this newest technology was a threat to our cherished profession, or whether it could be made to serve the study of literature and the development of literacy?

This book is about the answers we have found to our own questions. We have come to believe not only that we *can* do something about the effect of technology in our classrooms, but that we *must* do what we can to guide the development and direction of this powerful new educational tool. While telecommunications has added breathtaking new dimensions to the act of communicating, our focus on this technological medium has remained directed toward its uniquely human aspect—language as communication and as art.

Books

Everyone agrees that reading is an essential tool for learning, but it is far more than just a skill needed to acquire knowledge or information. Much more importantly, it is an experience that helps us discover how to live our lives to the fullest. It is through books that children encounter young people of their own age grappling with family relationships, substance abuse, peer pressure, and many of the other dilemmas they themselves face. Books enable children to break out of their own world, to dream, to come to terms with who they are and who they would like to become. Books make it possible for the poor and the affluent, the city dweller and the rural inhabitant, the young and old to trade places, at least for a time, and to envision a new way of being. Books bring us into the company of people whose cultures differ from our own, broadening our understanding of them and of our world. Books surround us with the beauty of language and give us words with which to share our ideas and our lives.

Books *can* do all these things and more, but only if we read them, think about them, talk about them, savor them. We spend a great deal of time teaching children to read and millions of dollars to improve reading test scores or to remediate children who fall below grade-level standards. But, important as good reading skills are, unless children read by choice, nothing will ensure that children who know *how* to read actually *will* read, not just in the classroom but throughout their lives. More than simply teaching reading skills, we must surround our students with good books and make reading an activity so pleasurable, so necessary to them, that reading and talking about books is as natural as breathing. In short, we have to help young people become true *readers* in every sense of the word.

Use of the computer may, at first glance, seem an unlikely way to transform reading—even for our most reluctant readers—into a pleasurable and lifelong activity. Children, however, have no "reluctance" about computers, which are for them an already natural part of the world. All of us know that relegating computers to a corner where students can play games once they finish their "real" class work or using them as a gimmick to do the same old, boring skill-and-drill workbook exercises is a waste of enormous potential. We believe, in fact, that computers can become a powerful force, one as powerful as books themselves became with the advent of printing, in creating the universally literate community of our dreams.

The Information Highway

What, then, is this "information highway" that everyone is talking about? The term suggests a fairly simple analogy—a major thoroughfare, with other roads leading into it, all connecting information "sites" with one another. The invisible highway itself seems to be a sort of yellow brick road that even the Scarecrow could use to find his way around the Land of Oz. But in this world of computer networks, the yellow brick road is a pathway of electronic signals, and "somewhere over the rainbow" is cyberspace rather than Oz.

When we first considered connecting readers on a computer network, what we wanted to know was *how* to use a network to enhance our teaching of literature and reading, not how to build one. We have happily left all questions of how the technology itself works to the electronic Wizards of Oz, whose help we acknowledge with heartfelt gratitude. What we have written is not a manual for mechanics, but rather a roadmap for *readers* who want to travel the magical highways of cyberspace.

The heart of the humanities, literature itself, is often lost in schools amid the rush to transmit information and skills. Reading books in the classroom is a "luxury" for which many schools can find little time or money. Educators estimate that children from primary through intermediate grades spend on average only about ten minutes a day reading "real" books. Yet recent research indicates that a key factor in developing reading comprehension is spending large amounts of time actually reading texts. At the same time, it has become apparent to teachers everywhere that students learn language arts more enthusiastically through the use of computers—a contemporary medium with which they feel comfortable. In a book-centered telecommunications project, children can choose both—computers *and* books.

The Challenge of Technology

Seldom in human history has a more profound change occurred than the one brought about in our time by the advent of the computer. As a result, we have a remarkable opportunity to make equally profound changes in the way we think about teaching and learning. Computers are not, as we once feared, replacing teachers—and computer games *have not* further reduced the literacy rate. In fact, word-processing applications have already been at least partially incorporated into more than 90 percent of high school classrooms, while nearly 50 percent of classrooms are already making some use of CD-ROM, multimedia systems, and networking (Stinson 23).

While lack of money and time are significant barriers to immediate and universal incorporation of computers and telecommunications into the English classroom, they are not insurmountable problems. Financial support will come as both government and business discover the imperative need. The Goals 2000: Educate America Act (**http://www.ed.gov/legislation/GOALS2000/TheAct/**) and the Technology for Education Act (**http://www.ed.gov/Technology**) are examples of the high priority Congress has placed on schools' use of technology. This legislation proposes major funding for a special Office of Technology in the U.S. Department of Education and for technology planning and implementation in every state. The debate of the day is not whether, but how, to provide access for *all* children, so as not to increase the inequities that already exist between the affluent and the underfunded school districts.

One major barrier does exist, however, in the lack of immediate, full-scale teacher training at all levels. Commitment to that necessary goal will require administrative vision and broad public support, already far too slow in coming. We cannot afford to wait. Teachers who want their classrooms to become the learning centers of the future will have to join now in educating those who can provide the means and those who will do so once the need and the values to be derived are understood. That means becoming knowledgeable ourselves, as fast as possible. It means pioneering, with meager resources and inadequate time. It means rediscovering the energy and resolve we carried into our profession. If schools really are going to be redesigned and education born anew, that rebirth has to begin in the souls and minds of teachers. When that happens, technology can be one of the means to that renaissance of the spirit in education which all of us want to see.

One of the most promising and most cost-effective ways to achieve an accelerated, nationwide teacher-training program in the use of technology for education is by means of the technology itself. With video and telecommunications linked, teachers can learn from the experts, take telecommunications courses, and visit virtually any classroom; they can share hands-on strategies, answer common questions, and solve common problems.

Our advice, based on our experience, is to plunge in now—but to plunge in with all the help you can get. Piecemeal learning can be frustrating and self-defeating. Find a computer-knowledgeable support person in your area, attend a workshop, learn the basics. If possible, use a team approach from the beginning, a collaboration among media specialists, librarians, teachers, and administrators.

A telecommunications project takes time, determination, administrative support, technological know-how, money, and a little magic. Any teacher who aspires to online teaching needs lead time—to develop skills and to develop, organize, and test computer applications in her own classroom. Administrators need to allow sufficient time and support well in advance, if teachers are to achieve the kind of success with technology that can lead to competence, confidence, and ultimately to educational breakthroughs for their students.

In this book we have provided a look at ways to use the nearly limitless possibilities of telecommunications as an educational strategy in the literature classroom. We have also included an extensive bibliography of additional sources you may wish to consult. We hope that what we say here will spark your own ideas of what you and your students might see and do on your way to the future of communication. When the information highway passes by your doorway, we hope this book will be your invitation to take to the open road.

We begin our journey with a project called BookRead. In Chapter 1 we shall take you with us on an adventure into the uncharted territory of cyberspace.

The BookRead Project

We have seen firsthand the excitement, involvement, and encour-agement this type of communication brings into the English class-room. Using telecommunications to teach literature can link students to other students, authors, and as a result, culminate in an educational explosion.

—Carla Beck and Shelley Sizemore, student teachers

The BookRead Project began in 1991 with the combination of two existing projects: WCU MicroNet, Western Carolina University's educational resources telecommunications network located in North Carolina, and the Fairfield-Westchester Children's Reading Project, located in Connecticut and New York.

WCU MicroNet, initiated in 1982 and brought to its present level with funding from the National Science Foundation, had been enhancing math and science education in North Carolina for ten years, using its electronic mail and conferencing features to facilitate communication among more than one hundred public and private schools, Western Carolina University, and other educational resources and agencies. WCU MicroNet was a resource base of teaching ideas, test banks, and general data retrieval. In 1991, it had just begun to serve as a similar resource in foreign languages.

The Fairfield-Westchester Children's Reading Project, launched in 1988 with funding from the DeWitt Wallace-Reader's Digest Fund, was serving 150 classrooms in Connecticut and New York, supplying them with newly published, hardcover children's books every month. The students contributed reviews to a monthly newsletter that went out to all the schools, as well as to booksellers and public libraries in the community. The students also voted on the books they read, and, at the end of the year, the project published an annotated list of "favorite books" for each age category. To further encourage the reading and studying of an author's body of work, the project invited authors into the classrooms throughout the year.

The co-founders of the BookRead Project, Marilyn Jody and Marianne Saccardi, met during the 1987–88 school year as participants in the Columbia University Teachers College Literature Project. Marilyn, who was at Teachers College as a Visiting Professor from Western Carolina University, coordinated the project along with Kathy Harwood, a children's literature specialist from New York University, and Lucy Calkins, director of the Teachers College Writing Project. Marianne had been selected as one of the fifty teachers from the New York area to participate in this year-long program.

In seven small reading groups, each with a leader experienced in conducting book discussions, the groups met weekly to discuss the adult books they were reading in common and to examine the latest in high-quality children's literature. Each teacher in the project was given more than forty books during the year's time to keep for her personal or classroom library.

By the end of the year, all of us in the project knew that our reading, our teaching, and our lives had changed. It seemed almost too simple. As the weeks had passed, through reading and talking together, we had discovered—or recaptured—the joy of reading and sharing good books. As teachers, we knew then that we had to create the same kind of opportunity for our students.

Before the end of that "Year of the Young Reader" (1989), Marianne had secured a grant to launch the Children's Reading Project and was supplying new children's books to fifty-three classrooms. Marilyn was developing courses which would be offered at Western Carolina University by computer telecommunications network, while she taught the same courses on campus at Teachers College. Eventually, the two of us began to see how the two projects could work together, in a venture we called "BookRead." Thus, we decided to run a three-week trial program.

Our plan was to bring book talk beyond classroom walls by having children in different parts of the country read good books and talk with each other about them over a computer network. We also thought we could bring authors online to appear in multiple classrooms simultaneously—on the computer screen. Again, it seemed almost too simple. But it worked. We asked Sue Ellen Bridgers and Gary Paulsen, two award-winning authors, to become pioneers with us, and although neither of them had ever used a computer network before, each agreed immediately.

The teachers we chose didn't have any experience with computer networks, but they were dedicated professionals who were already focusing on literature in the classroom and were willing to give the project three weeks of their precious classroom time. In the weeks before the actual project began, teachers and authors practiced using the WCU MicroNet system, sending each other electronic mail ("e-mail") and learning to transfer mail messages between their individual computers and the network (to "upload" and "download"). The high school students began reading Sue Ellen Bridgers's books, while the middle graders read Gary Paulsen's. At the suggestion of the students, the classes made and sent videos to each other, introducing themselves to their partner classes.

In the first week of the pilot project, teachers and students read and discussed their author's books in class and in their reading journals. We wanted the children to begin focusing on the ideas and questions they would be discussing with their partner classes, and we wanted the teachers to note how classroom discussions went in order to compare them with the computer conversations that would take place later.

During the second week, the students began writing to each other on the computer, taking to the screen with an ease their teachers envied. Some wrote general letters; others addressed specific students whom they selected as their pen pals. Teachers and authors read the conversations, amazed by the students' candor with each other, with their insights, and with their ability to influence each other's reading habits.

The authors opened the third week by writing sketches about themselves and their work. The students and the authors then exchanged electronic mail for the rest of the week. On the last day, all of the classes and authors were online simultaneously for a freewheeling chat. Student representatives typed their peers' questions and comments while the class viewed authors' responses on the screen.

Even before the stacks of copy from those three weeks were fully analyzed, we knew the BookRead Project was not only workable, but powerful. At wrap-up meetings and in follow-up letters, everyone was enthusiastic about what had happened. Christopher Renino, at Scarsdale High School (New York), wrote of his special class of "reluctant readers":

> BookRead worked beautifully with my students. The program did not miraculously make them avid readers, nor did it lead them to an overnight change in their attitudes about books, school, or themselves. However, they did read. Everyone read, and everyone read more avidly, in greater quantity, and more penetratingly than they had all year.

At Whitby School (Greenwich, Connecticut), Deirdre Fennessy said:

> One of the fourth graders was enthusiastic about using the computer to communicate to his peers and Gary Paulsen, and was silent when it came to talking about books in a group. For this student, the computer was an "equalizer."

In North Carolina, Melody Eury (North Buncombe High School, Weaverville) marveled at the results. She said:

> I was concerned that these students were reluctant readers. . . . One of these "poor" readers read every book we had—fourteen! One who never read a book at all last year read five.

The BookRead Project moved rapidly from that demonstration to an ongoing reality. A second project was conducted during May 1992, with seven schools in North Carolina and one each in Connecticut and New York. Authors Sue Ellen Bridgers and Jean Craighead George joined us for that project. The following school year began with a five-day workshop at the North Carolina Center for the Advancement of Teaching, funded by the North Carolina Humanities Council. Twenty-one schools from three states participated that year, along with authors Ann Turner, Cynthia DeFelice, and Sue Ellen Bridgers.

BookRead is now an ongoing project of WCU MicroNet, with multiple services for students and teachers, including an online continuing education course, "Teaching Literature Online," and three listservs on Internet: BR_Match, a BookRead Partner Matching service; BR_Cafe, a book discussion for precollege students; and BR_Review, a database of student-generated book reviews.

Primary grades through college classes have participated in our online literature projects. It has been fascinating to analyze their discussions, to discern how using the computer and providing a real audience has nurtured reading and writing, and to discover how our students' book talk can inform our teaching. Some samples can best demonstrate what happened, as well as some of what we learned from those online experiences.

Computer Conversations

A class of primary students, while tending eight eggs in a classroom incubator, read a book about a boy who finds a duck egg and hatches it at home. When these beginning readers wrote to their partners in another class about their reading, every single one of them typed a lengthy paragraph describing the plot of the book. Not one child talked about whether he or she liked the book, about the characters, about what they thought would happen, nor any of the other things people naturally say about the books they read. An opinion was hinted at by two students who used the term "great book" before writing the book's title in their letters.

The experience is probably a typical one, unless we begin early in the reading process by modeling "response." If we instruct children to tell their partners what the book was about, they will not write (nor say) what is natural to them. Although in this early example we were unable to see whether the partners responded and whether more advanced book talk got under way, we did learn from this one-sided conversation that students need to learn *how* to respond to books. We are convinced that even very young children can be taught how to do this. (We shall discuss techniques for the literature-based classroom in subsequent chapters.)

Middle-grade students in four classes in different states spent two months reading and discussing Jean Craighead George's books among themselves and with the author herself online. Teachers spent a good deal of time with these books in the classroom, and many of the children kept reading journals. Students were free to choose their reading material from a wide selection of books available in the room. In one school (Leadmine Elementary School, Raleigh, North Carolina) the principal became involved in discussing one of the books with the students, and several parents came in to work with them as well. A group of students studied one of Jean Craighead George's books about woodlands in the woods near their school. The two participating classes responded to the books they read orally, in writing, through varied activities, and by creating a mural depicting the animals they met in the author's books. One class even presented Jean Craighead George's *Julie of the Wolves* to another class. After all of this preparation, we were eager to see what these students would have to say to their partner classes in New York and Connecticut and to the author herself, who joined in these computer conversations.

Having been steeped in the literature, all of the students had a good deal to say about their books and wrote long letters to their partner classes. They listed the books they had read and their reasons for choosing to read them. They talked about the plots, the characters they liked, and the reasons why they did or did not like a particular book. Most often they asked questions—questions about what books other students were reading, whether they liked the books, and questions about the characters and events they read about.

Beyond these expected responses, the students, many of them as young as fourth grade, did some even more interesting things. One student associated George's *Shark Beneath the Reef* with Armstrong Sperry's *Call It Courage,* a book he had read over a year before.

Some students wrote about the author's craft:

The way she wrote, I could just picture what was happening in my head.

Every time Tomas dived [in *Shark Beneath the Reef*] I felt like I was there with him. I like feeling like I am in the story.

Jean Craighead George expressed herself [in *Moon of the Alligators*] like if she was seeing the alligator do everything.

Although the four participating classes never paired up as reading partners, they did write general letters back and forth. On one occasion, however, one child disagreed so strongly with another's response that she wrote directly to that student, the only instance in the two-month exchange in which one student specifically addressed another by name:

I read *Julie of the Wolves* too. I agree that it was a great book but it was NOT about "a girl named Miyax." It is about the wolves and how they acted and helped Miyax and adopted her and how she learned to talk with them and how she survived in the Artic [*sic*]. I really think you should read this book again.

Students often related the books to their own life experiences:

I like the desert one [George's *One Day in the Desert*] because I used to live in Arizona.

I really like the book. The whole idea of living inside the Catskills is so unique. In the same position, I would not do the same.

I just read *The Moon of the Salamanders*. The book has the best pictures in it. It made me realize how peaceful they are. I have a lot in the stream in my back yard. My dog trys [*sic*] to eat them but never gets them. Me and my mom go and catch them a lot.

One of the most powerful outcomes of these computer conversations was the students' ability to influence each other's reading—most forcefully felt, of course, in the exchange among our high school students. The students constantly asked each other what they were reading and recommended books. Some students who initially said they didn't like a book changed their minds when they were spurred on to keep reading by a peer:

I'm in the process of reading *Water Sky*. I like it a lot. It's about a part Eskimo, who goes to Alaska and goes on a right [*sic*] of passage. Have any of you read it? You should!

When I am finished with [George's] *Water Sky* I am going to read *Julie of the Wolves.* From the way people in your school described it, it looks pretty good.

Such comments are typical of these students' recommendations and their response to the suggestions of their peers. One student even looked to life beyond the two-month project: "After this project is over will you continue reading her books?" What more could a teacher hope for?

Most children enjoyed Jean Craighead George's books, expressing in their letters to her their pleasure in her work and proudly listing the titles they had read. The remainder of their correspondence was filled with questions. It was interesting to note that, even though the children knew what questions their peers were asking, they often asked the same ones and were not satisfied until they had received a personal answer—their own personal exchange with the author. Most questions had to do with how long the author took to write a book, where she got her ideas, whether she had ever experienced the things she writes about, and where her titles came from. But on a more personal note, one student asked, "What was the hardest thing to give up and to do? What is your future plan? What has been the most exciting thing that has happened to you?" Other questions were specific to the books—for example, why she had certain things happen, were events true to life, etc. But some children were brave enough to disagree with the author: "I have a comment for *Shark Beneath the Reef.* In it you said that Tomas's father was eaten by a hammerhead shark and in another book I read that hammerheads don't eat humans." Another wrote: "Why did you make the wolves nice? Most wolves are mean." Jean Craighead George was able to give all of these questioners satisfactory explanations (see Appendix A).

In reviewing these two months of computer conversations, the teachers were pleased with what had taken place. Certainly, the children had read and talked about books more than they ever had before. They were able to study one particular author in depth and become familiar not only with the content of her books, but also with her writing craft.

In reviewing what we had learned as teachers from this exchange, we felt these children might have had an easier time communicating with each other if we had paired them with specific partners or, since the numbers were not even, at least with groups. Some eighth-grade classes in North

Carolina who were engaged in another project exchanged reading responses in groups: "Cougars" to "Volunteers," "Historia" to "Untouchables," "Braves" to "Bearcats," etc. They were able to follow a line of questioning and to answer each other more directly, while the children in the Jean Craighead George project most frequently limited their responses to their own opinions or to asking questions. However, this experience with anonymous individuals in groups led to some verbal showing off and crude comments that required teacher intervention, an issue every middle-school teacher understands! Pen names must be used judiciously if anonymity is not to be abused as license.

Another project involved high school students: a group of students in the mountains of North Carolina and a group of disaffected learners in Scarsdale, New York. Of her North Carolina class, teacher Melody Eury said, "I teach a review-level class, and many of them have said that they *never* read (unless, of course, their grades depend on it!)." Chris Renino, the Scarsdale teacher, said, "My kids are generally not strong readers, and they have difficulty responding about writing." We wanted to see whether groups of young people such as these could be tempted by their natural love of the computer and by the fascination of communicating with distant peers from very different backgrounds to read more than they otherwise would and to write about their reading. Fortified with the books of two fine writers, Sue Ellen Bridgers and Gary Paulsen, and with computer labs at both schools, we began a two-month project which culminated in three weeks of online time among students, teachers, and authors.

The students began enthusiastically writing about themselves. Both groups were absolutely amazed by their vastly different lifestyles: "I can't believe you're getting married in June!!!" said one Scarsdale writer to his North Carolina partner. "Things are SOOOOOOO different here! How old are you? NO ONE here gets married until they're out of college. It's even hard to find a couple that's been going out for a long time (over 1 year)."

Letters told of their interests, from cars to religion, and even of one girl's leaving class for a few days to deliver her baby boy. These young people would have gone on for weeks in a pen-pal relationship, but we had limited online time and wanted to move them into book talk as soon as possible. Many of the students made no secret of their dislike for reading or for school in general: "I really hate reading! Really, really hate reading!

with a Passion!" or "I don't really care about school but to graduate" were common sentiments, expressed online without hesitation. Yet we asked these same students to read the works of two challenging authors, Sue Ellen Bridgers, whose books touch on many of the painful aspects of growing up, and Gary Paulsen, whose books about adventures in the wild appeal to many reluctant readers, especially boys.

As we observed the book talk in its initial stages, we witnessed students struggling with the reading process:

> I didn't like it [the book] too much, the author kept switching the narrator around, and it got really confusing. One paragraph would be the main character talking, then the next paragraph would be someone who has nothing to do with the story, talking. I hate reading to begin with, this just made it impossible to understand.

> I thought this book was kind of boring and it had too many details.

> I really don't have any more to say except the stupid book we have to read bites.

While many of these teens began by expressing their dislike for the books they were reading, constant feedback from one another began to change some of their outlooks. The most poignant transformation came about through A_'s (a girl in North Carolina) influence over M_ (a boy in Scarsdale). M_ began reading only reluctantly and told A_ a number of times how much he hated reading, and, in particular, how much he hated reading Sue Ellen Bridgers's *Permanent Connections:* "I don't like this book at all. It is too boring." But A_ began reading with vigor, finishing one book after another. And, either forgetting about how much M_ disliked reading or choosing to ignore his sentiments, she decided to provide him with a running commentary on her reading—all of it! For example, she gave M_ plot summaries and then discussed author style: "Paulsen pulls the person reading it into the drama of an adventure. . . . He tells what he saw in detail. Very much in detail. Details that make you feel as if it's you, that your [*sic*] seeing it happen with your own eyes." She gave her opinions and just kept on going: "I'm not through yet, I have yet another story to tell you about."

It wasn't long before M_ caught some of A_'s fire and was even willing to take another look at *Permanent Connections:* "I like Rob in *Permanent Connections* as a character because he faces real problems like all kids our age pot, pier [*sic*] pressure and drinking as shown in the book. He has trouble with his parents and rebels. I think this book was based on a real kids life." M_ had gone from hating the book, to discussing the main character, to relating events in the book to real-life situations. Reasons enough for teachers in both states to rejoice!

Like the younger students in our online projects, these teens talked with great honesty and enthusiasm to the authors of the books they were reading. They told the authors exactly what they thought, both positive and negative, of their books:

> The book itself was all right. But I think if there was more action, a lot more kids would be into it.

> To tell you the truth the beginning of the book wasn't that great. Then further in the book it got much better. The reason I did not like the beginning of the book was because it was dragging on constantly. I can tell I didn't like it since I read less than the required amount. There was a chapter when the book got really good. Over all from a 1 to 10 scale I gave your book a 5.

> Usually I really dislike reading. No matter what the author or what the subject. But there is something about your book that keeps me going. I am reading [Paulsen's] *The Crossing.* I like the way you started off the book in the first chapter! When I came to the second chapter I was puzzled by the relevance of it. I don't understand how it is in connection with the rest of the book.

> I had read the *Permanent Connections* book. I guess it was alright. You have to understand that I don't like reading too much. The only reason I kept reading was cause I wanted to see what kind of %*!# Rob was going to pull next. I really liked his attitude. He played things off that he could care less but inside he really had feelings and really did care what happened. I like that cause that is what I do. It's a great way to go about things. Sounds dumb but it works.

The students spoke to the authors as friends, often addressing them as "Gary" or "Sue Ellen," asking them personal questions and questions about their books. They even disagreed with some of the choices the writers had made in constructing their works:

> I found some things that the teenagers did in the book to be unrealistic. I did not like the way you described marijuana in the book. You made Rob sound like a crackhead just because he smokes a joint every now and then. . . . I also don't think you should let your publisher decide what your book covers look like. The cover of *Permanent Connections* was way off. That's practically fraud. . . . The only other thing I wasn't happy with in the book was the sex scene. I am seventeen and I think I could handle reading about Rob and Ellery having intercourse. So in the future at least make it clearer that your characters have had sex.

Everyone reading the screen that day—teachers especially—waited a bit breathlessly to see how Bridgers would handle this issue. She wrote:

> Dear D_,
>   . . . One problem is censorship, which is sometimes called the selection policy. That means a book that meets literary criteria can be eliminated from the school reading list because of something like describing sexual encounters explicitly. So there's a chance your school system would not have approved PC's use in your classroom because a parent or somebody might complain. I'm adamantly opposed to censorship but that's how it goes. Again, I guess my main reason for not writing more explicitly is that intercourse as a physical act isn't as meaningful as the passion that it evokes in the heart and mind. So I tried to describe that and leave the physical part to your imagination.
>   Peace,
>   Sue Ellen

It was a moment to treasure in a world that too often prefers censorship to wise mentoring.

While it was wonderful to have authors actually participate with us online, it is obviously not necessary to have the author of the books the students are reading join the project. One successful BookRead project, now in its third year, is a multifaceted study of the Holocaust among tenth graders, one group from a small rural Appalachian school and the other from a large urban school, both in North Carolina. Teachers Carolyn Franks (Andrews High School, Andrews, North Carolina,) and Diane Rutledge (Asheville High School, Asheville, North Carolina) created a world literature unit in which the topic, not the individual author, was the unifying force.

The project encompassed several requirements of the North Carolina state English curriculum and had, as one of its goals, to prepare students for the North Carolina State competencies test—a perfect example of integrating an online literature project into the established curriculum. The teachers chose several books, both fiction and nonfiction, poetry, and films as common experiences which the students would write about to each other. They took care to put students with similar work habits together to ensure a successful exchange. They also gave the students prompts for their letters, such as: "Write about an incident of discrimination and whether you were a victim, bystander, or perpetrator," or "Write about which book you liked best, *Night* [Elie Wiesel] or *I Was There* [Hans Peter Richter]." In response, the students' writing was quite focused:

> I liked *Night* better because it gave a better description of the concentration camps than *I Was There.* It told about how a boy lived through years of living in a concentration camp. He spoke of the horrors and life threatening situations that he had to go through. One occasion was where the Jews had to go through selection of being killed. He was told to run through as fast as you can so that you will look healthy.

> *Night* made me feel as if I was there experiencing the whole thing. The details were so graphic and terrifying.

> I can't imagine not being free. Just the thought of slavery scares me!! How about you? I can't imagine a second holocaust. I really hate the fact that the Nazis shot the babies as targets and you had to look at the people who were hung. That was awful. So how did the book [*Night*] affect you?

Because their schools were within driving distance, these two groups of students were able to come together at the end of their project for a talk by a Holocaust survivor and a viewing of the film *Schindler's List.* In all, it was a very thorough and satisfying several weeks. As one student put it: "I really would rather not read, but then I wouldn't know anything about the Holocaust."

Authors Online

We were fortunate enough to have authors Jean Craighead George, Sue Ellen Bridgers, and Gary Paulsen participate online with us in our study of their books during two separate projects. Their participation took several forms. Each author launched the project by introducing himself or herself to the children, writing some paragraphs about his or her life and work and sending them online to the participating schools. They read all the mail the children sent to each other so that they could have an idea of what the students were reading and thinking about. When letters were addressed to the authors, the authors responded. Both Bridgers and George wrote individual letters to each child, while Paulsen included answers to individuals in letters to the group. At the end of each project, the three authors engaged in an hour-long, real-time computer conversation with the classes who had been reading and writing about their books (see Appendix A).

Throughout the projects, the authors patiently answered questions, even questions that were put to them repeatedly. They were able to clarify issues, talk about their writing process, and provide insights into how their lives inform their writing. And just as students disagreed with each other and at times with the authors, the authors sometimes disagreed with each other: "The thing to remember, I think, when you read me," wrote Gary Paulsen to one group, "is that I write about what has been my life, what is my life." Both he and Jean Craighead George repeatedly told the children that the experiences they recount in their books are experiences they themselves had had in their own lives. Sue Ellen Bridgers, on the other hand, said, "Writers aren't limited to the events that happened to them. If they were, not many novels would get written." However, she also said that *Notes for Another Life* was a hard book to write because "my father had a similar mental illness and sometimes writing about that felt too close for comfort." In this experience, our students were able to see that the source of a writer's work is not an either/or issue, that writing is a complex process in which many influences play a part.

Our young readers were impressed with the care with which the authors responded to their letters. The online writing—particularly the authors' introductory comments—was oftentimes as well crafted as their work in books, and we often heard gasps of "Wow!" and "Cool!" when we read the authors' letters aloud. Children were awed by Paulsen's view of himself as a writer:

> I . . . love to write. I mean I really love it. The way you fall in love. When a story is right, when it cooks and comes right, the hair goes up on the back of my neck and my breathing quickens. I just flat love it. But if there was a better way to do it (for me), a way that worked better, I think I would do it. If I could put bloody skins on my back and dance around the fire and tell what the hunt was like and it worked better than sitting here typing, I would find the skins and light the fire.

We could almost hear the children's own breath quicken, and we certainly witnessed their renewed energy in their own efforts to put thoughts to paper.

Our students were also impressed by the authors' openness with them. The authors spoke of their childhoods, problems of mental illness and alcohol, parent interests that led them to a career path. They answered questions directly, never writing "down" to students, but rather addressing them as partners in the reading-writing process. Students let out a whoop of joy when, during their real-time chat with Jean Craighead George, she mentioned that one of them had just given her an idea for a sequel to one of her books. Jean followed through on that idea, and in the fall of 1994, her book *Julie* was published.

The authors never dismissed or trivialized student talk as irrelevant but accepted it as an indication of what was on their readers' minds; they respected these readers as persons. After batches of letters went back and forth in which the high school students talked about their cars, Gary Paulsen, in the natural course of talking about his dog teams and having to give them up because of his health, mentioned working on a 1953 Jaguar kit car: "I stuck a 289 in it with a hot cam and it's a little snakey." Perhaps it was the students' intense exchange about cars that prompted Paulsen to write *The Car,* the story of a teen who builds a kit car and travels west to find himself.

Students responded in kind, discussing their interests and feelings with an honesty that led Sue Ellen Bridgers to remark: "I'm sure glad I did an okay job of describing how smoking [pot] makes you feel. It's interesting that when I'm face to face with students, they never mention that. Maybe because they're with other people, including their teachers." Even though all of our classes knew that their teachers were looking in on their computer conversations, none of them appeared to feel inhibited, and even those who were shy in class offered their opinions freely.

While they offered technical challenges and some classroom management problems (it is difficult to keep all of the children focused when only one can type questions and responses into the computer), the online chats with the authors were project highlights. These discussions gave the students a chance to see an author's writing process in action. They were able to watch while an author stopped to think in midsentence or returned to an idea with additional comments. Through these discussions, students learned about the amount of time authors spend reading and writing. Gary Paulsen described how he schedules his day of writing:

> I get up at four-thirty in the morning, meditate for half an hour, then start working. Not always writing, but working. If I'm not writing I read and study and continue to study until I fall asleep.

They learned about the research and travel that go into Jean Craighead George's books:

> I spent long hours learning from the scientists at the Arctic Research Lab in Barrow, above the Arctic Circle.

They came to know how Sue Ellen Bridgers creates her characters:

> It's hard to write about people you know in real life because the real person gets in the way of the story, so I'm more likely to make up a composite person.

Bridgers shared even more about her writing:

> Actually, I write to accomplish two things, to tell the characters' story as best I can and to please myself doing it. While I'm writing, I'm not thinking about the reader much. Later, during the revision process, I try to make sure the story is understandable. That's when the reader is important.

Useful information for writers in the bud!

Teachers Online

Teachers have been among the greatest beneficiaries of our BookRead projects. The computer has enabled them to break out of the isolation of their classrooms and to enlist the ideas of their colleagues in helping their students become better readers and writers. Teachers talked to each other throughout the projects, analyzing their own students' letters, thinking out loud about ways to encourage reluctant readers and to enable their classes to become more focused. After a series of letters in which his students repeatedly stated that they disliked the books they were reading, teacher Chris Renino reflected in a message to Melody Eury:

> I have noticed how a student's mood on a given day can influence his evaluation of a book, even so far as to lead him to say something (i.e., negative, if that's his mood) when I know from other written work or a conversation that he doesn't really feel this way.

Comforting words for all of us!

Chris also talked about ways in which he was working with his students:

> I had my students do some more thorough preparation before writing. I think that perhaps that might be all it takes, in certain instances, to get them to say more than the first thing that comes to mind—"This book is stupid"—which is not always what they think deep down.

He suggested asking students to speak as "experts" on the book as a way to get them to say more.

Teacher Betsy Zellman (Leadmine Elementary School, Raleigh, North Carolina) planned activities for her students to engage in before they began writing online:

> We had special revolving workshops on *One Day in the Woods,* [*One Day in the*] *Desert,* [*One Day in the*] *Alpine Tundra,* and [*One Day in the*] *Prairie.* We had three parent volunteers and our wonderful principal Mike Jordan each take a book to teach . . . and we had my class teach *Julie of the Wolves* to [another] class.

Providing another advantage of an online study of literature, JoAnn Curtis (Language Learning Associates, Durham, New Hampshire), an educational consultant in the teaching of reading and writing, viewed the project from her computer screen and offered some ideas online in the teacher discussion area of the project:

> Is there a lot of [book talk] going on [in the classroom]? Are they getting a chance to see that talk written down? For instance, transcripts of a taped discussion? Might that provide a model of what good book talk looks like written down?

> Do these students in this project view themselves as writers? Do they write? Are they readers themselves? Are they examining their own lives, remembering, recalling, re-creating as Gary does in his books? Wouldn't you think that would make a big difference?

With help on all sides, from their peers and consultants in the field, our teachers were emboldened to go beyond established routines and try new techniques in this totally new venture.

Teachers also talked about their own reactions to the books. Writing to author Jean Craighead George, Deirdre Fennessey said:

> In *Gull* [*Number*] *737,* I could identify with the son who had surpassed his father in knowledge of the gulls' "loafing" patterns. It is not easy to believe in

oneself when your father does not believe in you. It is a necessary part of growing up, though, to proclaim your beliefs even though they may differ from your parents'. It is also painful, as Luke and his sister found out. Your story may help some of my students stand up for their beliefs when the time comes.

Teacher John Gibson [Whitby School, Greenwich, Connecticut], reflecting on Paulsen's books, wrote:

I am not a Gary Paulsen authority, but there seems to be a consistent theme running through a couple of books I have had experience with; that theme is coping with existence and death.

Reacting to Paulsen's *Hatchet,* Melody Eury wrote:

I couldn't put this book down! . . . A device of style I connected with is Paulsen's use of repetition. . . . The author uses "alone" three times in the last three lines of the chapter to let the reader feel the immensity of that fact for Brian (who is alone in the wilderness).

With good book talk like this flowing across computer lines, these teachers became models for their students and for one another.

Evaluation

At the completion of every project, we asked both teachers and students to evaluate what had taken place so that we might plan for the future. Teachers have been very positive in their assessments of the different projects in which they were involved. John Gibson told us that "the project created a community of readers and writers engaged in a common task; it presented a body of literature being read, written about, and discussed."

Many teachers shared John's view that the intense immersion in one author's body of work was an effective way for students to learn about the craft of writing. And these students did do some wonderful writing of their own in the course of the project. Looking over the letters that went back and forth, teachers could see that these letters sang with student voices in a way that other class writings did not. When they talked about how the project affected their students' reading, the teachers felt, as Melody Eury did about her student who read five books instead of none, that even those who did not like to read, read more than they otherwise would have.

The project also added a dimension that teachers and researchers alike found interesting. These students were not just responding to literature as they would in a reading-response journal, they were responding with an audience in mind, an audience that went beyond the boundaries of their classroom. Teachers Carolyn Franks and Diane Rutledge agreed that

> in writing personal letters to each other, they [the students] learn to adapt and accommodate someone else with different cultural or community values. Their ideas of discrimination practiced against them varied dramatically from one community to another.

Teachers also spoke about their own growth throughout the projects in which they participated. Teacher Mike DeVito (Port Chester Middle School, New York) wrote enthusiastically,

> I experimented with cooperative learning as I had never done before, I used the vast capabilities of word processing as I had never done before, and I challenged and observed my students immersing themselves in literature as I had never done before.

The Final Word

But perhaps it is best to let the children speak for themselves. One student wrote: "I enjoy learning with you [the online partner]. It's much better than textbooks." Another said: "This project got some people who ordinarily didn't read much to read a few of Gary's [Paulsen] books. I read *The Night the White Deer Died* and *Dogsong,* both of which I might not have read." And one enthusiastic youngster wrote: "The project was awesome! I started reading his [Gary Paulsen's] books (I wouldn't have otherwise) and now he's one of my favorite authors."

Teachers tell us that this enthusiasm continues even after a project ends. Book talk spills over from the computer into the students' lives. They continue to read and recommend books to one another. And having become aware through their conversations with the authors that books are written by living, breathing human beings, students recognize their kinship with these authors and use them as mentors for their own writing—big dividends from such a relatively small investment of time and energy!

Networks and Literature

In the BookRead Project, teachers discovered the exceptional potential of networking for improving both literature and literacy education. Person-to-person communities of readers and writers, teachers, students and authors connected across state and regional boundaries have helped to erase provincial barriers of regionalism, ethnicity, and economic status. Local communities have enhanced reading and literature education at a reasonable cost by having authors "visit" multiple classrooms through computer telecommunication. Teachers, children, and even parents have entered the new world of computer telecommunications together through the BookRead Project. Students have become more enthusiastic readers through meeting contemporary authors and other readers like themselves.

These children have increased their cultural awareness by getting to know their peers in other schools and other regions, as well as by reading good books. They have grown in their ability to respond to literature and to express their responses in writing by practicing these skills in an informal, real-world environment. The direct exchanges between young readers and their favorite authors have demonstrated clearly that good books themselves are the best motivation for reading and writing, while computers make writing a natural mode of communication for today's students.

The Classroom

2

Dear Gary Paulsen,
I like reading your books because they always end right. What I
mean by that is some books are good until the end. Then they make
the end so unrealistic that it ruins it. Yours aren't like that or at least
not the ones I've read. I've read these books of yours: Hatchet,
Woodsong, Dogsong, Dancing Carl, The Crossing, *and* The Winter
Room.

—Lynn, a fifth grader

Whether we teach in a self-contained elementary classroom or are responsible for a single subject in middle school through university, as teachers we are all too well aware of the limits of time and the limitlessness of the task. At national conferences we have heard leading educator Donald Graves lament that teachers have such demands placed upon them that many give in to employing a "cha-cha-cha" curriculum on the dance floor of the classroom, flitting from subject to subject in short quick steps in an effort to "get it all in." And with talk of even more national and state requirements finding their way into the curriculum, it seems clear that we cannot fit much more into the limited amount of time we have with students. If there is anything teachers do *not* need, it is another "add-on" program, however beneficial it may appear. Our first goal, then, in this book, is to show how to integrate an electronic-mail project into what we are *already* doing in the classroom, using the computer as a tool to accomplish our goals far better than we could without it. Thus the schedule we discuss below should not be seen as allowing a confiscation of several weeks from that which we must accomplish in the classroom, but as encouraging enrichment of what we are already doing *in* the classroom during those valuable weeks, by adding to our own perspectives those of the students, teachers, and—sometimes—authors who are now an actual part of our classroom reading and research community via computer network.

In a recent editorial in the *New York Times,* author Saul Bellow stated, "The literacy of which we are so proud often amounts to very little. You may take the word of a practicing novelist for it that not all novel readers are good readers" (A25). Reading results in learning, in exploring new ideas, in innovative applications only if our students understand what they are reading. With greater demands than before being placed upon them, with "higher standards" as common buzzwords throughout the educational community, we realize that we must bring our students beyond merely reading words on the page to critical understanding of what those words mean. In the past, we have given them various standardized tests to measure their comprehension skills. We have spent many classroom hours asking comprehension questions after they have read stories or chapters. What we propose here is not spending additional time on reading skills, or, conversely, ignoring skills altogether for more "meaningful" instruction. Instead, we suggest that classroom time be reallocated, from time spent on drills or testing to time spent on dialogue about books. It is a simple but powerful shift in emphasis. The K–12 students we have worked with in the BookRead Project read more books, with greater understanding, than ever before, as we illustrated in Chapter 1. Because they became invested in the computer network exchange, they were eager to make sense of what they were reading in order to communicate their ideas to their distant reading partners. And, as an added bonus, they tried harder to use conventional spelling and grammar so that their writing would be understood—and, in fact, did so competitively, so that their school would not be embarrassed!

Arranging a Schedule

A first step in setting up an online project is to schedule a time in the school year when you and your students can most easily set aside several weeks (six weeks is a realistic time frame) for a computer dialogue with another class. We have found that one project in the fall and another in the spring is a comfortable goal. With your school calendar at hand, try to eliminate times when you know your class will be pulled in other directions—for a school play, testing weeks, holidays, big sporting events, etc.

Choosing an Author or a Topic of Study

Once your time frame is established, your next task will be to find an author whose books you feel will "hook" your students and get them asking for more. Or, rather than focus on a single author, you could target a topic that you and your students have decided to investigate during the year and gather a variety of books on that topic for study and discussion over a computer network. As Byrum and Pierce emphasize in *Bringing Children to Literacy: Classrooms at Work,* this does not mean devising a neat unit of study to be used to teach other areas of the curriculum, but rather devising one that is genuinely entered into by both students and teacher, one which uses the other areas of the curriculum to investigate the subject at hand. In these authentic learning experiences, the class becomes a community of learners who are working for a common goal, who are courageous enough to take risks and to delve into material which stretches their capabilities. For these students, the curriculum is not something imposed on them, but rather a course of study they and their teacher work out together as they plan what they want to discover about a topic as well as what kinds of research and activities they want to pursue. The classroom becomes a busy, happy place where children are active participants in their own learning. When that learning is informed by literature, and when that literature is shared and discussed with another class engaged in the same study, the insights and learning are multiplied many times over.

For example, a class might express an interest in whales. Many books, both fiction and nonfiction, picture books as well as novels, are available to use, both to provide information for your investigation of these fascinating creatures and to fuel online conversations with a partner class. In his novel *The Hostage,* Theodore Taylor poses the question of whether a killer whale should be captured and sold to an amusement park or allowed to remain free. A Japanese mother tells her child the story of a woman who rescues her daughter from the underwater home of the whales in *Okino and the Whales* by Arnica Esterl. The excitement of going on a whale watch is recounted by Frances Ward Weller in *I Wonder If I'll See a Whale.* A lonely old man waits for the yearly migration of orcas and imparts his love of whales to his granddaughter in Sheryl McFarlane's *Waiting for the Whales.* Young children can practice their counting while being enthralled by Ed Young's beautiful illustrations in Tony Johnston's *Whale Song.* Some of the best nonfiction writers for children have written books on whales: *All About Whales,* by Dorothy Hinshaw Patent; *Great Whales, the Gentle Giants,* by Patricia Lauber; and *Whales,* by Gail Gibbons are just a few. Myra Cohn Livingston has selected poems about whales by leading poets for her collection *If You Ever Meet a Whale.* Older children may enjoy Shulamith Levey Oppenheim's *The Selchie's Seed,* about a young girl, descended from the Selchie folk, who becomes fascinated by a mysterious white whale. You can read some of these books aloud, or any others you might select, depending on the ages, abilities, and interests of your students. Students can also read and study others, individually or in groups. What children glean from these books—the questions they wonder about or the ideas they form as they read them, as well as the activities and investigations (perhaps their own "whale watch") in which they become involved during their study—is the "stuff" of their computer conversations.

Even when we feel that we don't have much room to make choices in what we teach because of curriculum constraints, we can still fill our lessons and discussions with literature and share what we are learning with other students online. Consider what you are required to teach during the year in all the disciplines. Is there a period in history that must be covered in class which would be enriched by historical fiction and authors who write excellent books on the subject for young people? Is an especially gripping science topic scheduled for study? There are a host of fine nonfiction writers for children whose writings would grace and enrich the science curriculum. High school English teachers who wish to undertake a computer project might consider the books their students are already required to read as part of the English program. Of course, these teachers cannot drop this core of mandatory books, but there are ways to work them into a computer project. The obvious solution would be to find a partner class which is reading the same books and engage in a dialogue with those students. Another possibility would be to find an author of young adult books who writes engagingly about the themes contained in the required books and to study that author's books to enlarge students' understanding of them. Or, teachers might want to consult their colleagues in the history or science departments to set up a team-teaching approach. The more you can integrate a computer project into what you or your colleagues are already doing, the less burdened you and your students will feel, the more support you will receive from other teachers in the building, and the greater the impact such an experience will have on all concerned.

Try to give your students as much input as possible in choosing an author. After all, they will be spending several weeks of their time, both at home and in school, reading and discussing that author's work. The more they feel a part of the decision-making process, the more enthusiastic they will be about the project. What authors are their favorites? Which ones would they like to know more about? Which genres do they enjoy or which ones do you wish to teach in a given term? With the incredible increase in books of poetry for children, anthologies as well as collections on special subjects, you might want to consider a poetry project for one term and a fiction study for another. Folklore is another genre rich in books for children of all ages.

Your Partner Class

It is important that you find a teacher whose class wishes to read the same books and who has a time frame that is compatible with your own. We will say more about how to find such partners, but for now, let's discuss some things you should keep in mind as you think about arranging a match. Again, it is important that your students join you in the decision-making process. Do your students want to write to a class as a whole, do they want to work in small groups, or do they want to be assigned an individual "pen pal" for the duration of the dialogue? Do boys want to talk to boys, girls to girls? Will teachers respond to students? To each other? Will teachers make their conversations with each other about the books available to the students? Will you want to invite an author to join the conversation? A computer discussion can take place very well without an author on board, but having one certainly does add interest. Do you have funds to pay an author to "visit" online? Can the cost be shared with a partner school or schools? Certainly, you would have to pay an author much less to engage in a computer conversation from the convenience of his or her home than you would to have that author travel to your school. Is there a local, regional, or national network link available to you that might supply authors?

Be sure to set up mutually agreed upon guidelines for the project with your partner teacher and class *beforehand,* so that all concerned know exactly what is required of them when they agree to participate. We have found that when a project falters, it is often because expectations were not clearly spelled out in the beginning. How long will the project run? When will it begin and end? How often will you exchange messages? How much teacher involvement will there be? How much conversation, if any, about topics other than the books in the project will be allowed? We have found, especially with high school students, that they are likely to talk at length online about their social and personal lives, often in response to reading-inspired topics. Students in BookRead Projects were fascinated with the idea that the kids they were talking to came from a different part of the country and had different ideas and customs. They wanted to air those ideas before they got down to the business of discussing books. And often these personal discussions became the link to their understanding of the books. For example, one young person who had confessed to his distant pen pal that he had family problems, wasn't trying in school, and had experimented with drugs changed his mind about how "boring" it was to read after he identified with the similarly troubled hero of Sue Ellen Bridgers's novel *Permanent Connections.* His comment was that the main character must have "been based on a real person."

It is important for both the teachers and the students to know in advance whether such exchanges are acceptable. Many classes we worked with made videotapes introducing themselves to their partner class before the online project actually began. These tapes were great fun to make, generated early enthusiasm for the project, and helped to build group cohesiveness. Some students even viewed their partner class's tape with the idea of choosing a particular student with whom to exchange ideas, while others preferred the excitement of anonymity.

Classroom Organization

If large chunks of your school day are already given over to reading and discussing literature, then you will not have many adjustments to make in your schedule or your teaching. You will continue to spend that time reading and writing, the only difference being that, in addition to sharing their ideas with one another, your students will also be talking to distant reading partners on the computer. If you do not have large blocks of time built in for reading and writing, some schedule rearranging must be done. Since students' lives outside the classroom are so busy, it is important to give them time in class to read and discuss books. While we expect them to read at home as well, the amount of class time we devote to reading and writing speaks to our students more powerfully than anything else can about our own priorities.

The Computer

In order for your students to begin their online computer discussion, it helps enormously to have access to a computer in your classroom. If you do not have one, perhaps a computer can be moved in for the duration of the project. Although it would be ideal (how often can we expect that?), this computer need not even have a modem or be connected to a dedicated telephone line. Students can simply use a word-processing program to make their comments and save them on disk at any time during the day that is convenient for them. Then, either at the end of each day, or a few times a week, depending upon how often you and your partner teacher have agreed to exchange messages, you can go to a computer that is connected to the

network and "upload" (copy and send) the text of your students' messages, along with your own. At the same time, you can "download" (copy from the network and save) messages from the other class to a disk and either print out copies for your students or have them read the responses on the computer screen back in the classroom. You can even do these uploading and downloading operations in the evening at home if you have a computer that enables you to do so.

Teachers who must rely on computers in another space, such as a computer lab or a library, have a bit more arranging to do, so the sooner you discuss your plans with others in the building, the more cooperation you can expect. Of course, the person in charge of the lab has to know about your project and be willing to work with you. If your class has scheduled computer time during the week, students can type their messages at that time. All the messages can be saved, transferred to one disk, and quickly uploaded to your partner school. If this sounds complicated, rest assured that it isn't. Have the media specialist teach you the few simple procedures involved rather than you having to rely on others whose time may not always be at your disposal. If you don't have enough computer lab time, you may be able to arrange to use another teacher's time in exchange for some of your computer lab time, once your project is completed.

While much of what we say here can apply to any classroom, we shall describe in subsequent chapters how the computer network can become a part of high school and college classrooms, where both space and time are subject to different kinds of limitations.

3

The Literature

The project created a community of readers and writers engaged in a common task; it presented a body of literature being read, written about, and discussed.

—John Gibson, teacher

In "What Computers Still Can't Do," recalling a half century of efforts to program computers to achieve "artificial intelligence," Hubert L. Dreyfus points out that "the field ran into unexpected difficulties." The trouble started, he says, "as far as I can tell, with the failure of attempts to program children's story understanding. The programs lacked the intuitive common sense of a four year old . . ." (4). He concludes that:

> Society must clearly distinguish its members who have intuitive expertise from those who have only calculative rationality. It must encourage its children to cultivate their intuitive capacities in order that they may achieve expertise, not encourage them to reason calculatively and thereby become human logic machines. In general, to preserve expertise we must foster intuition at all levels of decision making; otherwise, wisdom will become an endangered species of knowledge. (9)

Books are where we begin. Before we actually undertake a computer book discussion project, it is essential that our students be steeped in literature, that they learn to talk about books face to face as naturally as they talk about what they are going to do after school or about the latest baseball scores. But before they can have conversations about books, they need to be comfortable listening to and talking to each other.

Creating a Classroom Community

A real conversation happens only between people who care about each other. If this is true when the conversation is on familiar ground, how much more so when we are trying out new ideas, venturing into challenging books, coming to grips with different writing styles. It is important then that teachers spend a considerable amount of time at the beginning of the school year turning classrooms into caring communities of learners, places where students listen, not only to us, but to each other—places where it is safe to take risks without fear of failure and where each person's contribution to the growth of the group is eagerly anticipated. Shelley Harwayne, in *Lasting Impressions,* and Ralph Peterson, in *Life in a Crowded Place,* have written eloquently about the need to create a classroom community to support students in their efforts to learn. Many of their ideas are woven into the suggestions that follow.

The Classroom Environment

We can begin creating a classroom community by taking care with the physical setup of the room. "The way we organize our classrooms," states Regie Routman, "affects children's views of themselves as readers and writers and has an impact on their attitudes toward school and learning" (423). Children can sit in clusters at tables rather than in isolating rows. Area rugs and plants create a more relaxed atmosphere. Materials such as paper, pencils, and so forth should be accessible on shelves so that the children can obtain them independently. It is helpful to have children work together to decorate the room so that they have a vested interest in the space and its care. Shared spaces, such as the science center or the classroom library should be kept tidy so that everyone in the room can enjoy them to the fullest extent. We can give children a sense of responsibility as well as a sense of belonging by turning over to them, as much as possible, the upkeep of the room and the other necessary functions for the good of the group: class librarians for the library corner, milk money collectors, attendance takers, and so forth. Even very young children can be expected to clean up after themselves and leave a space in good condition for the next users.

A Community of Sharing

Community arises out of a common bond, something shared—family relationships, a neighborhood, a task, ideals, or goals. Shared stories can be a good place to begin creating a common bond in the classroom. Gather the students together on a rug or in a close space and let them in on who you are, what is important to you, your personal goals, and your desires for this particular class. Share stories from your childhood and your life at present. Students, too, need time to tell us and one another who they are, to share their family stories, their hopes and struggles. And they need time to practice being good listeners. Children are surrounded by so much noise in their lives that they have become masters at screening out sound. Hence, we cannot take for granted that they listen when we or other members of the class speak. Perhaps certain rituals during a sharing/listening time—lighting a candle, gathering in a circle, observing a moment of silence before beginning, keeping hands down while someone is speaking— will help children develop good listening skills.

As we share our literate lives with our students, it is important for them to tell us who they are as readers and writers. Educator Jane Hansen suggests that an effective way to do this is to ask them to prepare a "literacy portfolio," a large envelope or any suitable container in which they place articles that reveal their reading and writing histories. Anything may be placed in the portfolio as long as the student can explain why it is there. For example, a literacy portfolio might contain a favorite book or poem; a reading/writing notebook; a picture of a special place where an individual likes to read or write; a special writing pen or pencil; a stuffed animal to whom or with whom a child reads or has read; a picture of a person who has been or is a reading/writing mentor or with whom the student likes to read or write; forms that might indicate a child helps family members with literacy tasks—and, yes, even a particular floppy disk!

The possibilities are endless, and children will soon catch on if you model your literacy portfolio before they start preparing theirs. It has been our experience that sharing literacy portfolios over several days has broadened students' horizons as they experience the wide variety of literacies represented in the room, helps them bond to one another, and provides invaluable information for us about our students' reading and writing habits.

Shared tasks, both academic and practical, are another way to build community. Groups of children can work together to create a choral reading of a passage or a poem, to uncover layers of meaning by discussing a passage read aloud, to find the solution to a problem, to plan a unit of study, to create a poster or other work of art. When different groups in the room share their work, it is fascinating to see the variety of ideas and presentations that emerge even from the same task. There is cause to celebrate in this spectrum of talent and ideas. There is cause to encourage these individuals to come together in their learning so that we can all be enriched.

Even in a college classroom, where students might be expected to consider themselves far too mature for such projects, we have seen literature students, working in groups of four and five, write and publish (using desktop publishing) "newspaper" accounts of the writers and events from the period they had been studying. Each was responsible for contributions to the paper, in whatever form they chose—news, features, book reviews, even crossword puzzles, sports pages, and classified ads. The content and the display of imagination were both impressive, and students considered that particular assignment their "best learning experience" of the semester.

A Community of Diversity

Most of us have students in our classes from different ethnic backgrounds. Make time to celebrate who they are and to rejoice in the variety they can bring to the classroom. Celebrate feasts that are special for different groups. Invite family members in to share traditions and customs— "programs that respect the home and language of the child, building on this diverse base, open literacy to all" (Peterson and Eeds, 8).

Many children's books are available to help a class share in the rich heritage of its members. *Celebrating Hanukkah,* by Diane Hoyt-Goldsmith and *Ramadan,* by Suhaib Hamid Ghazi, help children understand the significance of these religious celebrations to those among their classmates and others who observe them. *Grandfather's Journey* is Allen Say's Caldecott Award–winning recollection of his Japanese grandfather, torn between his love for Japan and his love for the beautiful landscape of America. Neil Philip's selection of Native American poems in *Earth Always Endures* can help readers appreciate the wisdom and traditions of Native American peoples. In *Harlem,* Walter Dean Myers traces and rejoices in the African American migration to the streets of New York City. Hispanic culture is reflected in more and more books for young people. Among them are outstanding offerings such as Tony Johnston's *Day of the Dead,* Elizabeth King's *Chile Fever,* and Gary Paulsen's *The Tortilla Factory.* The poems for older children in Gary Soto's *Canto Familiar* honor large and small moments in the lives of Mexican Americans, while his picture book *In Chato's Kitchen* treats younger children to an unusual Mexican feast. Sherry Garland's novel *Shadow of the Dragon* acquaints older students with Vietnamese customs while at the same time revealing how difficult it is for young people to live between two cultures. Grace Hallworth's *Down by the River* is a collection of lively Caribbean rhymes and chants. Emery and Durga Bernhard describe how mothers of different cultures carry their babies in *A Ride on Mother's Back.* In *My Song is Beautiful,* Mary Ann Hoberman has selected fourteen poems that view childhood from a variety of cultures. Written in the first person and illustrated by different artists, the poems in this collection each celebrate a unique culture and heritage.

Because many picture-book versions of folktales are published each year, it is fairly easy to find tales from our students' countries of origin. Reading these tales can spark discussion about ethnic customs and encourage children to share other stories with which they are familiar.

Regardless of our students' ages or ethnic backgrounds, we can find books to help them reflect on their roots and rejoice in who they are.

A Community of Readers

If we want to create a community of readers and writers, then we must be models of reading and writing ourselves. In "Classroom Environments for Reading and Writing Together," Nathan and Temple state, "Your students need you to read books you choose, and for you to become famous, perhaps infamous, for talking 'books' in the teacher's lounge, at your dining-room table, at the parties you go to. Shed your 'I've no time' skin—if you're someone who needs to—and take time, make time, to read" (Shanahan 182).

We must read, not just texts that will help us prepare social studies and science lessons or manage a classroom, but all kinds of books, fiction and nonfiction alike. "What are you reading now?" is a question we are asked all the time by our students, and they expect us to have an answer. From time to time we can read aloud appropriate passages from adult books we love, lingering over beautiful language, pausing to voice our questions and wonderings. And, of course, we can fill our students' lives with wonderful children's literature in a variety of genres in daily read-aloud sessions. "The sharing of literature aloud anchors the sounds of the language of literature in the minds of the students" (Peterson and Eeds 8). They begin to speak and write and think in the language of books. Isabel Beaton, a teacher in New York City, tells the story of a four-year-old who, while Isabel was serving her class breakfast, put a grape on his spoon, held the spoon aloft, and walked solemnly up to the front of the room saying, "Abuelo de la noche" ("Grandfather of the night"). Because Isabel makes literature the air her students breathe daily, this little one had taken the language of Barbara Berger's picture book *Grandfather Twilight,* in which grandfather carries a pearl in his hand and tosses it into the night sky, and made it his own. Children who hear stories read aloud daily begin to love and treasure books, to become passionate about them in much the same way that, as author Norma Fox Mazer says, "Americans love ice cream." They have "a passionate involvement, [a] willingness to try all flavors, a lighting of the eyes, eating it in all seasons, a pint always in the freezer" (27).

Several years ago, Marianne Saccardi spent some weeks reading E. B. White's *Trumpet of the Swan* aloud to a group of first, second, and third graders. Together they agonized over the death of the old cob and cheered for Louis as he learned to write and eventually won the heart of his desired mate. They marveled together at his cleverness in getting a job and overcoming the many obstacles he had to face as a mute swan. A short time after they had finished the novel, Marianne received a phone call at home. "A terrible thing just happened," said a very sad voice, which she immediately recognized as seven year old Morgan's, on the other end of the line. "I just heard on public radio that E. B. White died." They talked for a bit about how sorry they were and marveled together at the wonderful things White had accomplished in his more than eighty years of life. "Well, anyway," Morgan concluded, "we'll always have his stories." By building a repertoire of shared literature, we give children a common fund of stories upon which to draw all year long. They will return to these books and poems and stories again and again for ideas, a perfect word, and, as Morgan did, to recapture enjoyable moments spent at the feet of a master writer.

Choosing and Acquiring Good Books

There are probably as many definitions of a "good" book as there are readers, but there are some characteristics upon which most people involved in the study of literature can agree. A good book is one that holds the reader's interest throughout, one that draws the reader to close gaps in understanding by making his or her own meaning from the text. If there are a sufficient number of gaps in the work, the reader stretches himself or herself to a new level. If there are too many gaps, the book is probably too difficult for the age or ability of the reader and should be put aside. If there are not enough gaps, then the book is too easy, too predictable in a pejorative sense, or too formulaic to be compelling and should also be abandoned. A "good" book has the power to transform lives.

Over 4,000 children's books are published every year. Add these to the huge body of work currently in print, and it is clear that selecting just the right book for a particular child or class can be a formidable task indeed. Fortunately, there are many journals that provide teachers with fine reviews and timely articles about using literature in the classroom. *School Library Journal, The Horn Book, The Bulletin of the Center for Children's Books*, and *Booklist* are just a few of the publications teachers can turn to for help. In addition, there are numerous sites on the World Wide Web that contain reviews of recent books and lists of notable and other award-winning children's books. These sites are listed in Chapter 7.

Knowing what to look for in a good book can make selection easier. And if we are familiar with some of the wonderful books that have maintained the respect of reviewers and have been beloved by children and adults through the years, then we also have models against which to judge the new books we encounter in our search.

When we select fiction for children, it is important to consider such elements as plot, setting, theme, characterization, style, point of view, and format. Is the plot new and original (or a well-used plot with a new twist) or contrived and predictable? Does the setting have an impact on the characters and the story? Does the author do a good job of creating a lasting impression of the setting without bogging down the book in details that are tedious to children? Is the setting believable, even in a work of fantasy or science fiction? Is it evident that the author has researched a particular time well and has included details that bring the reader into that time and place? Is the theme or message of the book handled subtly, or is it didactic and heavy handed? Does the book, regardless of the sad events that might occur within its pages, leave young readers with the feeling that life will go on and that the characters will endure? Do the characters stay with us long after the book is closed and the details are lost to memory? Are they real and believable? Are their thoughts and actions in keeping with what the author has told us about them? Do the characters grow and change, or are they well developed? How? Does their dialogue ring true? How does the author write? Is the language memorable or stilted? Do the words sing? Who tells the story—the main character? A third-person narrator? Do we agree with the author's choice of point of view? Is the book well designed? Is the print large enough, the white space in proper portion, the size of the book right for the age of the children reading it? What about the shape of the book? A picture book about trees that has a tall thin shape, for example, says something about its subject by its very being, even before we turn the first page.

Particular kinds of books need special consideration. In choosing picture books, of course, we need to pay particular attention to the illustrations. Do they develop and enhance the story? Does the medium chosen convey the mood of the story? For example, watercolors with their transparent quality achieve a very different effect from thick brush strokes done with bright acrylic paint. What about color, line, space? Nonfiction books should be judged on the accuracy and timeliness of their information and on how knowledgeable the author is about the subject. Has the author studied extensively in the field? Does the author show evidence of a passion for the subject, a passion that, as noted nonfiction writer James Cross Giblin said in a speech given at Columbia University's Teachers College, "makes the book as emotionally involving as fiction, perhaps more so." Does the author have a degree in the field? Has he or she written other well-received books on the subject or in other nonfiction areas?

Good fantasy and science fiction often have layers of meaning hidden beneath an involving plot. Jane Yolen, a prolific writer of fantasy for young people, states,

> Life Actual tells us that the world is not perfectly ordered. Endings are as often unhappy as happy. Issues are seldom clear-cut. Judgment is as capricious as justice. Babies starve and there is no resurrecting them. Mothers die or run off and are never found. Families are torn asunder and there is no mending them. And honesty is rarely the best policy when it comes to exposing your friends. But Life in Truth [fantasy] tells us something else. It tells us of the world as it should be. It holds certain values to be important. It makes issues clear . . . And so the fantasy tale becomes a rehearsal for the reader for life as it should be lived." (*Touch Magic* 64)

Works of fantasy need to be filled with accurate details and be consistent and believable.

Above all, we must trust ourselves. If a book comes alive for us, if it holds us, haunts our quiet moments, calls to us to be read again and yet again, then that is a book we must share with the children in our lives.

Although budgets have been scaled back in most school districts over the past few years and school libraries and librarians have often been high on the list of cuts, most schools do have a central library. However, it is important to have classroom libraries as well. Certainly, we can and should send our students to the library to do research, to hunt for books by an author we want to study, to search out writing ideas. But when we have books right at hand (ten to twenty books per child is a good number to aim for in a classroom library), we are more likely to weave literature throughout the curriculum, to pull a book off the shelf to illustrate a genre or style of writing, to encourage reading. Children have an ever-present reservoir to draw upon for ideas, inspiration, and enjoyment. And, most important of all, a room filled with books speaks more eloquently than we ever could about the central place of literature in our lives. Literate adults, while frequenting their public library, surround themselves with books at home as well. The children in our classrooms deserve the same literate atmosphere in the place they inhabit for so many hours each day.

Hardcover children's books are expensive, but there are ways to acquire them even on a limited budget. If at all possible, request classroom library funds from your school. Perhaps some PTA money can be used for this purpose. Involve your students in raising money for their classroom. They can run a bake sale, a car wash, even run errands. If they are involved in earning the money for their library, they will value the books all the more. Once you have money in hand, there are ways to make it go further. A number of book distributors or jobbers sell books at substantial discounts. Book clubs such as Arrow, Scholastic, and Troll sell books at exceptionally low prices. They usually offer only paperbacks, but these clubs are a good source of multiple copies for group discussions, and a way for students to build inexpensive home libraries of their own. Teachers also get points for free books for the classroom when their students order the required number of books.

There are also ways to get books without funds. Elementary school children can write letters to the local high school asking the older students to check their attics and bookshelves for children's books they have grown out of and no longer wish to keep. We can peruse our local library from time to time to see if any of the books they are discarding would be useful in our classrooms. Garage sales frequently offer good books for as little as twenty-five cents. Wherever we get books, however, we must make sure that the books we put into our rooms are in good condition and are quality literature. A free book in good condition that is badly written or illustrated is not a treasure. On the other hand, an excellent book that is dirty or torn beyond repair is not a treasure either, and it gives the wrong message to students about our reverence for books. While not being suitable for the classroom library, however, books in poor condition can often be put to other uses—pictures can be cut out, paragraphs can be put on overheads to illustrate the writing craft, and so on.

A Community of Writers

Students, especially those who are asked to write daily, expect us to be writers, too. Teachers who write know what it is like to face a blank page or computer screen, to grapple with the difficulty of putting ideas, seemingly so clear in their heads, onto paper in a way that others can understand and enjoy. We teachers should let our students know about the kinds of writing we do—stories, letters, articles, poems, lists, reports—the kinds of writing that come into our homes. What letters do we treasure from family and friends? What kinds of mailings do we receive from corporations, even from organizations soliciting funds? When appropriate, we can share writing we are currently working on, asking for our students' suggestions in places where we are stuck. We can ask them to help us hear whether the words we have chosen are just right.

Children who are fortunate enough to be surrounded by literature have a rich fountain from which to draw ideas and language for their own writing.

> As if holding up an intricate shell to hear the sounds of the ocean, a young child listens to the sound of story. The murmur of kings and queens, courage and destiny, rhythm and rhyme, new and strange vocabulary flows into her mind. When the story is over and the voice in her ear ebbs away, the child is left with a residue of the treasure.
>
> In the child's mind one story combines and recombines with other stories, connecting text with text and text with life. A child who moves easily in and out of the pages of a book carries a full spectrum of stories in her head. She links texts together, creating a weave of books with everyday life, using the senses of sight, sound, and movement to uncover and explore common theme." (Wolf and Heath 705)

We often ask our students to write about what they know, to write about themselves and their families. Studying a group of authors who have written autobiographies or memoirs can provide our young writers with excellent mentors for this type of writing. Beverly Cleary, in *A Girl from Yamhill*, and its sequel, *My Own Two Feet*, Jean Fritz, in *Homesick: My Own Story*, Eloise Greenfield, in *Childtimes*, Trina Schart Hyman, in *Self-Portrait: Trina Schart Hyman*, and Jean Little, in *Little by Little* give their young fans insights into their lives and how they ply their craft while at the same time showing them how to weave the bits and pieces of their lives into an interesting story.

James Stevenson, in *Don't You Know There's a War On*, and Deborah Kogan Ray, in *My Daddy Was a Soldier: A World War II Story*, give readers a vivid picture of what it was like growing up in America in wartime, while Milly Lee tells a similar story from a Chinese American's point of view in *Nim and the War Effort.* A very different picture of those war years is presented in *Bad Times, Good Friends: A Personal Memoir* by Ilse-Margaret Vogel, the author's account of how she and some of her friends survived the Nazis in Berlin. In *Chalk Doll,* Charlotte Pomerantz tells her mother's story about a doll she had as a child. The young narrator in Tony Johnston's *How Many Miles to Jacksonville* describes the thrilling arrival of the train, "steam rising through the pecan trees," sparks and cinders spraying "in one long hush," at the Jacksonville, Texas, station in the early half of the twentieth century. In *Grandmother and the Runaway Shadow,* Liz Rosenberg tells the story of a grandmother who takes a shadow along as comfort and company when she leaves for America in the middle of the night to escape pogroms against the Jewish people in eastern Europe. Annie's great grandmother, grandmother, and mother all married water-men and lived on Chesapeake Bay through good times and bad as described in Barbara Mitchell's *Waterman's Child.* Neighborhood residents gather nightly to hear family stories in Sandra Belton's poignant *From Miss Ida's Porch.* These and so many other picture books and novels can serve as models for children who are trying to write well about themselves and their families.

Literature can help children reach into all the corners of their lives for stories of their own. When we share picture books that deal with the trials of getting up in the morning, meeting a new friend at school, visiting grandparents, going shopping, and so many other small moments that make up a life, we enable our students to see that topics for their writing can come from anywhere, and that they need not have done something "monumental" in their young lives to have material for a story. Shelley Harwayne, in *Lasting Impressions,* and Lucy Calkins, in *Living Between the Lines,* write extensively about having students keep notebooks in which to capture the seemingly insignificant as well as the larger slices of their lives. In these notebooks they record the events of the day, family happenings, ideas from their reading—anything that touches them. They try out stories. They carry their notebooks with them wherever they go, ready to jot down what they see and hear, much as an artist always has a sketchpad handy. When they get ready to write a story that will go from draft to finished published piece, they thumb through their notebooks, underlining kernels, images, impressions, ideas that really matter to them, anything that has the potential to be fleshed out into longer pieces.

Because the children about whom Harwayne and Calkins write have been steeped in the stories of literature, they find topics everywhere, and having found topics, they look to literature once again to decide the form their writing will take—a picture book, a poem, a letter, a short story, a memoir, and so on.

While literature can help our students choose writing topics they really care about and decide what literary form is best suited to those topics, it can also help them learn the "how" of good writing. A story or poem or any other form of writing is much more than a good idea. It is *how* that idea is expressed that matters, that makes us want to turn the page and keep reading. There can be no better teacher than literature itself. Marc Aronson states, "Words are some of the first gifts we give to children. And in books for children, not only do we use words to tell stories, the words themselves are a continual enlargement of the child's world" (*School Library Journal* 30). When we read stories written even by very young children, it is easy to recognize those writers who have been exposed to literature from their very earliest days. They are comfortable with the written word and, like marvelous Max in Rosemary Wells's delightful *Bunny Cakes,* confident that they can express themselves on paper. These children use the language of stories in their writing. They often begin "Once upon a time . . ." They use words and images that surprise and delight us—language they have assimilated from their reading. Children who know the pleasure that a carefully chosen word can bring are those who follow the sheriff across the desert as he tries to rescue Sweetness until he becomes so tired he's "feelin' like somethin' that was chewed up and spit out" in *Saving Sweetness* by Diane Stanley; who "show off [their] fancy footwork" as they go "bopping and shoowapping" with the animals in Vic Parker's *Bearobics*; who cringe as a "smug slug" ignores "sinister signs" and approaches certain danger in Pamela Edwards's *Some Smug Slug.* These are the children who clap to the rhythms and rhymes of poems; who marvel at the surprise of viewing the moon as a "mirror in heaven" in the Tang poem "Moon" from Minfong Ho's *Maples in the Mist*; who love the image of a tiny dancer complete with "white tie, top hat, gold-tipped cane" to express the sound of rain dripping on a porch in James Stevenson's poem "The Dancer" from *Sweet Corn;* who watch "the waves in their snow-flower capes bend at the waist and come tumbling in" in Barbara Juster Esbensen's poem "Dance-line at High Tide" from *Dance with Me.* These are also the children who are willing to play with language in their own writing.

We can use literature to help our students understand how to write authentic dialogue. Avi has written his novel, *Who Was that Masked Man Anyway?,* using only dialogue. What a challenge and what an excellent model to put before students who are trying to get their characters' words just right! When we read descriptions such as Thomas Locker's view of the sea as the "cool silver moonlight sparkles and dances on [its] waves" in *Water Dance,* or Carolyn Lesser's metaphor of the desert as a "great bowl" ready to be filled with rain in *Storm on the Desert,* or the Arctic river, "shimmering and humming, as it awakens from its icy winter sleep, in Nancy White Carlstrom's *Raven and River,* then we can encourage students to see with new eyes as they describe people and places in their own writing. Books such as Gary Paulsen's *Work Song* and Catherine Cowan's *My Life with the Wave* illustrate how some stories come full circle. Students can discuss how authors develop characters, and they can read about some unforgettable people, both in picture books such as Kevin Henkes's Lilly's *Purple Plastic Purse,* and in novels such as Gail Carson Levine's *Ella Enchanted.*

Nonfiction writing in the content areas makes up a considerable portion of the writing we require of our students. So often when they write reports or essays, their writing takes on the impersonal tone of an encyclopedia. If the major source of information for their work *is* an encyclopedia, then we shouldn't be surprised. Perhaps one of the most dramatic changes in children's literature today is the wealth of attractive and well-written nonfiction books available for students of all ages. James Cross Giblin writes with authority and passion about such unusual topics as unicorns, Santa Claus, the Rosetta Stone, even chairs and windows. Readers know from the very first page that this author cares so deeply about the things he chooses to write about, that he finds ways to make his subjects interesting to others as well. In his many nonfiction books for young people, Seymour Simon starts with what his readers know to help them assimilate information about the world around them. "Make a fist," he urges readers in his book *The Heart: Our Circulatory System,* so that they will have an idea of the size of their own hearts. In *The Brain: Our Nervous System,* he enables readers to "follow a single message as it moves through millions of nerve cells from [their] finger to [their] brain." Dorothy Hinshaw Patent, Caroline Arnold, Sandra Markle, and Jim Arnosky are just a few of the authors who write enticing, well-researched books about animals and nature. If we make good nonfiction available to our students and help them see that such writing can take many different forms—picture books, poems, plays, letters, diaries, and so forth—there will be a marked difference in the quality of their work.

Author Studies

In *Lasting Impressions,* Shelley Harwayne talks about authors serving as children's mentors in their writing. Engaging in an online computer project is a wonderful hook for encouraging students to study an author deeply for an extended period of time. Choose an exemplary writer like Cynthia Rylant, for example, whose writings have been honored by the Caldecott and Newbery committees, who has written a wealth of both picture books and novels, and who is an excellent model for children of all ages to study in depth. Rylant's works are outstanding examples of writing at its best: from her "Henry and Mudge" books, which serve up humorous and practical solutions to problems faced by young children everywhere; to her delightful "Mr. Putter and Tabby" series; to her glimpses of life in Appalachia, in *When I Was Young in the Mountains* and in *Appalachia: The Voices of Sleeping Birds;* to her poignant collections of short stories, *Every Living Thing* and *Children of Christmas;* to the dreams of Solomon Singer, in *An Angel for Solomon Singer;* to a young boy trying to find God, in *A Fine White Dust;* to a young girl trying to find love and come to grips with her aunt's death, in *Missing May.* Gary Paulsen, Sue Ellen Bridgers, Avi, Kevin Henkes, Eloise Greenfield, Gary Soto, Betsy Byars, Lois Lowry, Katherine Paterson, William Steig, Mem Fox, Vera Williams, and James Stevenson are also among the many fine authors who have a body of work large and varied enough to interest and instruct children. If an author has written in more than one genre, in both poetry and prose, for example, he or she offers even more opportunities for study.

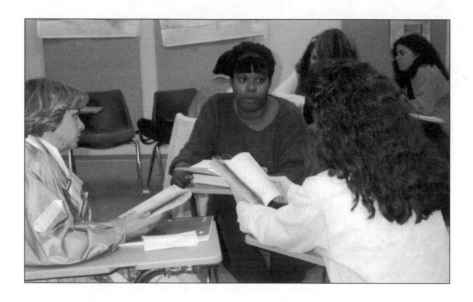

Begin an author study by gathering as many of that author's books as possible. You might want single copies of those books you plan to read aloud to the class and multiple copies of some titles the entire class or groups of children will read and discuss together. Involve the students in the search for books as well. Read aloud every day from works of the author being studied. Appropriate paragraphs from adult books, if the author has also written these, might also be considered for reading aloud.

Once you have a collection of books at hand, there are a number of things you might look at. The themes or content of the books is the most obvious. What does the author most frequently choose to write about? Why does he or she write about these things? Do the stories come from childhood, from grandparents, from the part of the country in which the author lives? Find out as much as you can about the author's life so that students can see how life informs art. One of the first places to look for information about authors is the Internet. Many well-known authors have their own Web sites. In addition, there are children's literature sites that offer information about, or links to, authors and illustrators who create books for children. Many publishers also have sites that provide information about their authors. Chapter 7 contains a description of some of the most interesting and helpful Web addresses for those interested in books and authors. Most libraries have a set of books called *Something About the Author,* which contains biographical information on the most popular authors writing for children. Publishers are also excellent sources of biographical information. Most of them have brochures, often written by the authors themselves, on the authors they publish. These brochures contain valuable information not only about the author's life, but also about why and how he or she writes. For those who teach high school students, there is a CD-ROM called *Discovering Authors* that provides biographical and critical information on 300 authors of American, English, and world literatures. In the book *Authors' Insights: Turning Teenagers into Readers and Writers,* edited by Donald R. Gallo, such outstanding young adult writers as Robert Cormier, Harry Mazer, Norma Fox Maxer, and Chris Crutcher write about themselves and their work. Another fine series of autobiographies is called *In My Own Words.* These stories, written by authors of books for readers in the middle and upper grades, are well told and certain to give students insights into writers whose books they have come to love. Some of the autobiographies in this series include *The Moon and I,* by Betsy Byars; *The Invisible Thread,* by Yoshiko Uchida; *The Lost Garden,* by Laurence Yep; and *Anonymously Yours,* by Richard Peck. Adolescents will also enjoy noted author and illustrator Ted Lewin's account of how he earned money to attend art school in *I Was a Teenage Professional Wrestler.* The *Meet the Author* series is an excellent source with some author biographies for very young children. Titles in the series so far include *Best Wishes,* by Cynthia Rylant; *A Storyteller's Story,* by writer and storyteller Rafe Martin; *A Letter from Phoenix Farm,* by prolific children's author Jane Yolen; *A Bookworm Who Hatched,* by the noted reteller of folktales, Verna Aardema; *Surprising Myself,* by Jean Fritz, who is famous for her highly readable and entertaining biographies for children; *Playing With Words,* by James Howe, the author of the Bunnicula stories; *Hau Kola = Hello Friend,* by Paul Goble, a writer of Native American folktales; *Firetalking,* by Patricia Polacco, author of many multicultural stories; *The Writing Bug,* by well-known poet Lee Bennett Hopkins; *Once Upon a Time,* by Eve Bunting, author of over 100 novels and picture books; *Thoughts, Pictures, and Words,* by children's poet Karla Kuskin; and *My Mysterious World,* by

Margaret Mahy, an author from New Zealand. These books are short, easy to read, and real treasures for teachers who want to involve even the youngest readers in an author study. Another fine account for the picture book set of an author's road to publication is Helen Lester's *Author: A True Story,* in which she describes how she overcame a disability to become an author. When children read that Cynthia Rylant nourishes herself on the works of Randall Jarrell, Donald Hall, and E. B. White, and that her main concern is "what really, really fine literature sounds like" (Antonucci 29), they know why her own choice of words is so precise that her stories sing. When young lovers of the "Frog and Toad" books can hear Arnold Lobel say, "I believe I have to try . . . to write truthfully out of the middle of myself, to work out of the sadness and, of course, the joy" (Antonucci 29), they can begin to realize that their own stories must come from the middle of who they are as well. When they read that well-respected author Richard Peck believes "writing isn't self-expression. It's communication" ("Nobody But a Reader" 80), they will see the value of trying and trying again to be clear on paper. Of course, if your class is fortunate enough to have an author involved in a computer project with them, they can talk to that author directly, ask what inspires him or her to write, question parts of stories, and learn firsthand what goes into the creation of a book.

It is important to go beyond *what* authors write to the *craft* of writing. *How* do they do what they do? What kinds of sentences or paragraphs do they write, long or short? What about their use of dialogue? Who most often tells their story—one of the characters, a third-person narrator? What about their choice of words? What is it that makes an author's voice or style so unique that we recognize it when we hear it, much as we recognize the voice of a favorite pop singer on the radio even if we haven't heard the song announced? Children need to read and hear and discuss many books to discover how an author plies her craft. And the discoveries can grow in ever-widening circles if students have the opportunity to share what their peers in other classes in other parts of the country have uncovered about an author they are studying. While all of this study is enormously interesting and even fun, it is very time-consuming. So we have to take steps to ensure that the information our students gather will actually become part of their writing repertoire. Harwayne suggests that we cannot take it for granted that our students will automatically use the techniques they have learned from author studies in their own writing; we have to give them a "gentle push" to get them to imitate the authors they admire. We can encourage them, even orally, to begin a story as a favorite author would; we can challenge them to write a few paragraphs in the voice of an author they have studied. If they can do exercises such as these, then the best of what every author has to offer can become assimilated into their own writing. They will learn to read as writers, asking themselves, as Harwayne suggests, whether they too can "do that."

Teachable Moments

As we have described in this book, a good deal of preparation and hard work goes into making an online book discussion happen. When we first began these projects, we rejoiced that the students in our partner classes were, indeed, talking to each other—and that they were actually talking about books! We celebrated when students enticed one another to read books they might not have chosen on their own. We delighted in the many ways the students learned from each other and from the authors who spoke to them online. But as we continued to review transcripts of these computer conversations, we began to see yet another dimension. If we, as teachers, pay close attention to what our students are saying about books and to their responses to their partners' comments and to the authors in our projects, these conversations can serve as a blueprint for our teaching. We can determine what our students need to know in order to become better readers and writers. To illustrate what we mean, we share some excerpts from a recent computer project that linked students in Alaska, North Carolina, Connecticut, and Indiana with each other and with author Jean Craighead George. In this project, we had three sets of partner classes, each set talking to its own partner and to the author. As a culminating event, each set had a real-time online conversation with Ms. George.

A Tie-in with Social Studies

We discovered early on that students were fascinated by the locales and lifestyles of their peer partners. Students in Atlantic, North Carolina, were eager to tell their correspondents in Alaska:

> We made a snowman for the very first time. School was out for us. We don't
> have snow equipment to clear the roads because snow is so unusual. Our
> mean temperature ranges between 68 and 72 degrees.

On the other hand, the students in Alaska wanted to clear up some misconceptions of folks in the "lower forty-eight":

> We don't live in sod houses in the summer. We don't live in igloos . . . Many
> people like to use the white man's cultural things . . . We don't make caribou
> skin sleds with frozen reeds. We don't rub noses . . . We don't use kayaks to
> hunt seals but wooden and aluminum boats instead.

While hearing from students in places as far apart and different as Barrow, Alaska, and the coast of North Carolina would certainly increase students' curiosity, we have observed this same desire for cultural exchange in group after group of students over the years. What is the climate like? What school activities do they participate in? What kinds of cars do they drive? What are their plans after high school? Taking our cue from the students, then, it would make sense to begin an online book discussion project with a study of the area in which the partner class lives, and to encourage more personal exchange at the outset until the students feel comfortable with one another. We have found that once this initial information is digested, the actual book discussion becomes more focused and satisfying.

Following a Line of Conversation

We have found over the years that students, in their eagerness to express their own opinions or to ask their own questions about the books they are reading, often fail to "listen" completely to others online or even to the author. Consider this transcript of a conversation among two classes of students and author Jean Craighead George.

> From Ipallok School in Alaska: "Mrs. George, which of your books took the
> longest to write?"

Jean George: "It took me the longest time to write CRY OF THE CROW because I didn't like some of the characters and kept trying again."

The next comment online was from a student in North Carolina:

"What is the title of the first book you published?"

The author had given the students a valuable insight into her writing process—how she struggles until she creates characters that please her. The students could have followed up on this initial statement by asking Jean what she didn't like about her characters and why, how she changed them, and so forth. Yet they went off in an entirely different direction. We have witnessed lost opportunities like this over and over again in online conversations. Instead of probing a topic to its depths, students continue with their own agendas. We advise teachers to solicit volunteers to engage in a "fishbowl" type of discussion in the front of the room, while the rest of the class observes and takes notes. Were the participants really responding to one another, or making their own isolated comments? What contributed to the successes or failures? What advice would they give the participants for future discussions? Then divide the class into discussion groups, assigning an observer to each group. Did the groups succeed in following a line of conversation? Why or why not? Only after such preparatory experiences will the students be ready to engage in an online book discussion, where distance and the computer screen create even more challenges than a face-to-face exchange. The potential benefits to be gained from such in-depth responses make the preparation for them well worth the time and effort.

What Do Good Readers Do?

As more experienced language users, we teachers need to help our students make meaning from the authors' words in the books they read. An effective way to do this is to reflect on what our students are actually saying about their reading and lead them from there to explore other aspects of a book. Transcripts of computer conversations can become a rich source of information.

Listen in on what one group of students wrote to partners across the country:

> Now we are going to tell you about chapter 1 in *Julie of the Wolves.* Miyax (Julie) left her home on Nunivak Island and headed toward San Francisco to visit her penpal Amy. On her way she got lost in the Artic [sic] wilderness, without even a compass. She eventually ran into a pack of wolves. The first one she met was named Amaroq. At first, the wolves didn't trust her but later on she became trust worthy, and they feed [sic] her caribou. We predict that Julie will not make it to San Francisco.

In this comment, the children simply summarize what they have read. They do make a prediction but give no evidence from the text to substantiate it. Plot summary is, of course, the easiest kind of book discussion for students, and they can engage in it without our help. However, for them to benefit more fully from the riches good books have to offer, they need the vocabulary to talk about these books and knowledge of the many facets of a literary work. They need to know it is desirable to talk about their own reactions to a book and the reasons for them. They need to know that one can bring a discussion of plot to a new level. Does the plot work? Is it believable, interesting, unusual, too predictable, filled with suspense? How does the author assure that the reader will stay interested to the end? What is the book truly about—what is its underlying theme? Can we predict what will happen based on what we know about the character's traits, about interactions with other characters, about what has happened so far?

Students need time, practice, and, above all, modeling, to be able to engage in book discussion at deeper levels. We advise teachers to participate in the online book discussions along with their students, labeling what they say with such opening statements as, "I'd like to talk about how the author made me really believe Julie was adopted by the wolf pack." Or "I'd like to talk about how the author developed the theme of friendship in this book." In this way, we help students know the kinds of things it is possible to talk about in a book discussion, and we give them the vocabulary they need to do so. We also encourage teachers to have students keep a reading notebook and to have them write in it before going online so that their comments to their partners stem from what they have been thinking and questioning as they are reading. Teachers can model types of entries and ask open-ended questions that prompt students to probe an aspect of the book more deeply. Of course, when students or the author bring up interesting topics, we can put their comments on overheads and talk about them.

Developing Characters

Character development is such an important aspect of a novel that we look for every opportunity in online conversations among the students and authors to call attention to it. A student from North Carolina wrote, "Julie is a good character, because she learned to talk to the wolves, she was confident in herself, and she was brave to go back to Kapgun's [sic] house." Author Jean Craighead George replied: "You are interested in Julie's character. That is what all good novels are about—character." What a wonderful opportunity for follow-up classroom discussion! Students can find sections in the book in which the characters through word or deed reveal what they are like, and they can share these passages with their partners online. What does the author do to make us care about a character in a book? Students can turn to the author herself for more enlightenment. And, fueled by what they have learned from their reading, they can try to flesh out the characters in the stories they write themselves.

The Author's Craft

Throughout the project, Jean Craighead George encouraged the students to write: "You all have wonderful stories right around you—in the mountains of North Carolina, on the tundra of Barrow and indoors with your family and friends. Get yourself a protagonist, a setting, and start writing what is happening around you." In focusing on the author's craft, students discover how to use words well in their own writing. Over and over again Jean gave the students glimpses into her writing process as she responded to their questions and comments. These were moments to treasure and to use to full advantage in the classroom. "I like how you make story characters have emotions and it seems like you're right there when it happens," wrote one student from North Carolina. The author responded:

> Your observation that you were right there when it happens is the comment I am most proud of. I like to think my talent is bringing each reader right on scene. To make them see the landscape, the characters, be part of their lives. If you think I have done this I am very happy.

This exchange might be followed by a discussion of things an author can do to bring readers into the story as well as a hunt through the book for places in which the author does just that. The students can ask her about these scenes. How did she write them? What was she trying to accomplish?

As we read student comments like, "The best part for me is when Julie is lost on the tundra and met Amaroq and the pups, because it was exciting . . .", we encourage them to dig deeper. What is exciting about this scene? How has the author created this excitement? Are there other places in the book that readers find exciting? Why? Discuss these scenes with partners online. Did they have a similar reaction to them? Why or why not? Have the students ever attempted to create exciting scenes in their own writing? Did they succeed?

When one student wrote, "Julie of the Wolves was a good book . . . I thought that the author used great describing words. She put in many similes; for example, on page 34: 'but he was like water, and slipped through her hands,'" we had students select and read favorite descriptive passages throughout the book. Eventually, reading about Julie's wolf pack prompted some descriptive writing about dogs, and we were delighted with results like the following:

> My brother has a dog named Jake Mendoza Stevens. He is about seven months old, and he is a full breed Pit Bull. He is about the size of a teacher's desk.

Of course, students need to know that getting the words right isn't always easy, and Jean told us this in different ways over and over again: "I write and then I rewrite. Sometimes I put a manuscript away and start all over again." Teachers can encourage students to discuss this topic further with the author. Can she show them "before" and "after" examples of a rewritten passage? What makes the rewritten version better, stronger, more interesting? Pair the students and have them discuss various drafts of their own writing with one another. How can these drafts be improved?

The Role of Research

Sometimes students believe research is necessary only when we write non-fiction. How valuable, then, when an author makes a comment like this: "I read a scientific article about the wolf society, their leaders, their language, their devotion and knew I must write about them. So I went to Barrow, Alaska, to study and be with wolves." It presents an opportunity to talk about the role of research in writing; the importance of getting right such facts as climate, vegetation, and so forth; the value of keeping a writer's notebook in which to jot down information learned for possible use in a story. Students can ask the author how she conducted her research. Did she interview people, read, have a guide help her learn about wolves? Which students have found they needed to do research for their own writing? How did they go about it? What might help them in the future?

Getting the Most Mileage from an Online Reading Project

An online computer project may only last a few weeks, but it can enrich your literature program all year long. We follow up with additional studies:

1. Are there other authors who write about the same topics or in the same style as the one we have studied in this project? What can those authors teach us?

2. What have we learned about reading and writing by participating in this project? Teachers might wish to process this learning with the students and to put some ideas on charts for display in the classroom.

3. Are there additional aspects of reading and writing we wish to emphasize throughout the year? Can overheads of comments by the author or students online help with the discussion?

4. Are there follow-up activities suggested by the author's books or comments? For example, students in this project talked to Jean Craighead George about her views on keeping animals in zoos. This conversation might be followed up by letters to zoo administrators asking about the care and treatment of animals, a visit to a zoo, or even a study of a particular zoo animal.

By focusing on "teachable moments" during and even after an online computer reading project, we can extend the learning far beyond the computer screen. And if partner teachers share what they are doing in their classes with one another, the opportunities for enabling our students to become better readers and writers know no bounds. We hope that those of you who engage in such projects will share your ideas with us as well.

Computer Conversation Basics

4

If we could blend electronic images with great teachers and books, and use computers as learning tools, America could, in the next century, have the most outstanding educational system in the world.
—Ernest L. Boyer, Carnegie Foundation for the Advancement of Teaching

Teacher Commitment

At the heart of any successful literature program in which computers are to play an integral part is a teacher who first believes it is essential for students to read and talk about books. That same teacher also must be confident that the computer can be an effective way to bring readers and writers together in meaningful dialogue. Without this conviction, it will be difficult to commit the amount of classroom time that an online book project entails, or to stand up to the challenges involved in launching something new.

An online discussion of books simply means being connected to others in your reading community by electronic network. Networks can consist of two computers, linked to each other in the same room or building (a local area network or "LAN"); or millions of computers linked to each other around the world (a wide area network, or "WAN"). An online book-discussion program will require time on your part to become familiar with an electronic mail system, if you are new to the technology; time to choose and read a set of books and prepare students to engage in the project; time to set up a partnership with another class—and possibly with an author as well; time to arrange a schedule; and time to conduct the discussion both in the classroom and on the computer.

Additionally, the teacher who leads an online book discussion must become actively involved in reading and talking about the books and in working on the computer. Watching from the sidelines as the computer teacher takes over the technical side of the project will not work. Technical support staff are a great asset and should, of course, be working with you. But we have discovered that, in schools where the classroom teacher does not learn how to use the system, momentum dies down, partly because computer personnel cannot devote enough time to one particular class when they are faced with the needs of an entire building. But even more important is the effect teachers can have on student involvement. Enthusiasm is catching. In our workshops with teachers, we devote half of each day to hands-on work with the computer.

Books and Authors

We cannot assume that children automatically know how to talk about books. We must explain, model, and allow time for good book talk in the classroom. Teachers modeling what it is that good readers do and what they talk about with other readers, student-teacher dialogues, small reading discussion groups, reading partners, and reading journal entries are just some of the many ways teachers can facilitate book talks.

Because students need to be invested in their reading, they should be able to choose for themselves, from a variety of titles available in the room, the books they will read individually. It is also important to have a common reading experience that can form the basis of discussion about an author's work. The teacher should read some of the author's books aloud. Small groups of four or five students can also read and discuss the same book. In order for you to be able to provide such varied experiences for your students, it is important to choose an author who has a large body of work in print. This may seem like a tall order, but at least you don't have to limit your choices to authors who live close by, as you might when arranging face-to-face author visits. And knowing where to look can make the task much less difficult.

Begin with the obvious. Is there a children's author you particularly like or one whose books your students enjoy? Look in one of that author's recent books to find out what company published it and contact the publisher. Some authors write for more than one publisher, so be sure to check out several books. You need only negotiate with one publisher, but it helps to know what other publishers handle your author—especially where paperback books are concerned. A publisher of hardcover editions will not usually volunteer information about a book published in paper by a different house, and you might spend unnecessary dollars on a hardcover book when you could have obtained it in paper. Consult *Children's Books in Print* in your school or public library for this information.

When you settle on a publisher, ask for the children's marketing department and then ask if they have someone in charge of arranging author visits. Most publishers have someone who does this, but we are not listing names here since, in many publishing houses, people move in and out of that position often. The person who sets up author visits has usually worked with all the authors in the publishing house and can be very helpful. You can ask if the author you are interested in is comfortable with the computer. If you can provide instructions, many authors are willing to try e-mail, even if they have never used it before.

Be sure you know beforehand exactly what you would like the author to do and when you want him or her to do it. For example, would you like the author to introduce him or herself in a few paragraphs on the computer before your students start reading? Would you expect him or her to answer mail every day, once a week, a few times a week? How many students will be writing to the author and expecting answers? Is a group answer sufficient, or will you expect the author to answer individual children? Do you want the author to engage in a simultaneous online discussion with your students and a partner class for an hour or so toward the end of the project? How many weeks will your project last? What are the exact dates? Can you be flexible, to fit into an author's schedule? Because many authors work against deadlines, it is important for them to know precisely what they are being asked to agree to and how much of their time it will take.

Since no travel time is involved, and the author can probably answer e-mail in the evening when the writing day is over, you can usually negotiate a price that is far lower than what you would pay for an in-person visit. And there are no travel expenses, hotel bills, or meals for you to provide! Usually, the marketing person has to check with the author. If the answer is "no," he or she may be able to suggest someone else for your consideration. Make sure to finalize everything in writing, and take advantage of all the services the publisher can offer you. Many publishing houses provide book jackets of the author's books to entice your students into reading them. They also can provide a list of all the author's books as well as biographical information, leaflets, bookmarks, and so forth. Some publishers even have videotapes of their authors speaking about their work. Publishers will also sell you the author's books at a 30 to 40 percent discount. Once the publisher and you agree on a price and dates, they will probably make the author's address and phone number available to you and you can continue your planning with the author firsthand.

If you do not have an author in mind, there are a number of ways to find out about the people who are currently writing books for children. Publishers usually print two catalogs a year, one that contains the books they are publishing in the fall and another for the spring list. These publications are wonderful sources of information. They contain biographical information about the authors who have books coming out during the season and information about the forthcoming books as well as other books the author has written. Illustrators are also featured. You can request free catalogs from any of the major publishers. In addition, many publishing houses have kits featuring authors and illustrators who enjoy becoming involved with schools. Contact the Children's Book Council for a listing of children's book publishers (see the "Reading and Writing" section of the "Additional Resources" bibliography).

Often professional magazines—*The Horn Book, The Instructor, The Reading Teacher, Teaching K–8, The New Advocate, and the ALAN Review* are just a few—contain articles by children's book authors and illustrators or feature interviews with them. Reading these articles and interviews can provide you with valuable insights into an author's thinking and methods of creating books and may help you decide whether he or she is someone who can teach your students what they need to know about reading and writing. Occasionally, authors go on tour, appearing in children's bookstores, libraries, or at conventions. If you have the opportunity to go to such an event, you might be able to approach an author personally and determine his or her willingness to participate in a computer project with your class.

One of your greatest resources is your school librarian or the children's librarian in your public library. They know which authors are popular with children, which ones write quality literature, and which ones have a body of work large enough for your purposes. And, if at all possible, invite your students and the teacher and students in your partner class to join you in your search for a suitable author. The more invested students are in the project, the more successful it will be.

Basic Equipment

Computers can be the least expensive components of the project. In fact, since computer technology changes so rapidly, there might be businesses in your area that would gladly donate computers to your school as they upgrade their equipment. Even unsophisticated computers can handle electronic mail. What may have become outmoded in the business world can suit your purposes very nicely.

Along with the computer, you will need a modem, the instrument that converts computer language into telephone signals, for electronic transmission. Some computers come with internal modems; for others, a modem must be purchased separately. These too can be acquired at a very low cost. And a telephone line is required, preferably one that is "dedicated," that is, used solely for the computer connection. A dedicated telephone line can cost several hundred dollars to install, but after this one-time expense, monthly use charges are generally reasonable. When you weigh these costs against the thousand or so dollars it would probably cost to bring an author into the school for a face-to-face visit, the cost of a telephone line that enables you to bring into the school electronically not only many authors, but the whole world, can actually look like a bargain.

You will also need a connection to a network, perhaps one in your school or to a local or regional area network to begin with, and later a subscription to a larger telecommunications network. If your telecommunications connection does not make use of an 800 number, you may have to budget for long-distance charges. Many local and regional network connections are available to schools, either free or at a very low cost (see Chapter 6 for a discussion of network connections).

In his practical discussion of how schools can overcome budget limitations (see Appendix D), Randy Pitts writes that "used and refurbished systems can go a long way toward filling in the technology gap many schools face." According to Pitts, IBM, Apple, and GE have all entered the "remarketing" industry, where computers that can meet school needs more than adequately are priced thousands of dollars below market cost for new equipment. (See the next section, "Funding," for ways to support technology.)

Vicki Hancock and Frank Betts of the ASCD Education and Technology Resources Center suggest multiple ways to put technology in the teachers' hands, including rent-to-own agreements; options to do professional work in places other than the school; provision of teachers-only electronic tools in the schools; installation of a telephone line in every classroom; and technology loan programs for teachers' home use (24–29).

Funding

The effort to bring the information superhighway to every classroom in the country at a cost we can all afford has become a national priority. Funding for bringing technology into the schools is available from any number of sources, from government to business to charitable foundations. Federal funding for technology in the schools received its biggest boost in 1997 when Congress approved the first year of funding for the President's proposed five-year, $2-billion Technology Literacy Challenge

Fund. States have been asked to revise their Goals 2000 plans to include the four goals of this initiative:

1. All teachers will have the training and support they need to help all students learn through computers and through the information superhighway.
2. All teachers and students will have modern computers in their classrooms.
3. Every classroom will be connected to the information superhighway.
4. Effective and engaging software and online resources will be an integral part of every school curriculum.

A number of other major federal funding opportunities have recently emerged as well, including the Universal Service Fund under the Telecommunications Act, to enable schools and libraries to purchase at a discount any telecommunications service, internal connections among classrooms, and access to the Internet; statewide NetDay events to wire schools and classrooms; and the 21st Century Teachers initiative, recruiting 100,000 teachers nationwide to voluntarily train 500,000 more teachers on how to use computer technology in the classroom. For information about these and other federal initiatives, you can visit the Department of Education Web site at **http://www.cd.gov/Technology/.** You can also consult the annual *Catalog of Federal Domestic Assistance,* available at your local library or from the Government Printing Office.

Among corporate funders, the AT&T Learning Network has made a $150-million commitment to support educational technology, including $50 million in grants by the year 2000. For information visit the AT&T Web site at **http://www.att.com/learning_network/.** IBM, another major corporate funding source, offers $10 million in gifts of technology and cash awards through its Reinventing Education Program. The Web site for Reinventing Education is **http://www.ibm.com/IBM/IBMGives.** For a comprehensive listing of private foundations and corporate giving, The Foundation Center publishes *The Foundation Directory* and the *National Directory of Corporate Giving.* Online you can reach the Foundation Center's exceptionally useful Web site at **http://fdncenter.org/.**

Many journals for educators, such as *Electronic Learning, Learning and Leading With Technology,* and *Technology and Learning,* publish ongoing lists of sources for funding technology in the schools. Keeping up with funding opportunities is also made easier by a number of newsletters on the Internet. For example, *The Education Technology Monitor* is a good new source of information about funding, available from the Education Funding Research Council at **http://www.grantsandfunding.com.** *Education Technology News* is another excellent online source of up-to-date funding news, available electronically by subscription from Information Access Co. at 1-800-321-6388.

The schools we have worked with have used various means to obtain necessary funding when the regular budget was already fully committed: a small grant from a local business, PTA funds, even a student fundraiser. Imagination and initiative can lead to many avenues of unexpected support. A useful guide in this regard is *Obtaining Resources for Technology in Education: A How-to Guide for Writing Proposals, Forming Partnerships, and Raising Funds,* by David Moursund, from the International Society for Technology in Education (ISTE). *The Educators' Internet Funding Guide: Classroom Connect's Reference Guide to Technology Funding,* another helpful source that includes a searchable CD-ROM directory of sources, is available from Classroom Connect.

Staff Development

Nearly every study of technology in education points to lack of teacher preparation as one of the major current issues, reiterating what Vicki Hancock and Frank Betts write:

> To realize any vision of smarter schooling by using technology, school districts and colleges of education must prepare teachers to use the technology. Apart from funding considerations, adequate teacher preparation is probably the most important determinant of success (58).

A clear indication of the direction teacher preparation is taking can be found in new teacher-certification requirements around the country.

Accrediting agencies are examining teacher education programs to make sure preservice teachers are being trained for the classrooms of the future. And inservice teachers are upgrading their own skills, not only to meet new certification requirements, but also new curriculum requirements for their students. To examine your own state's K–12 standards and requirements in technology, visit the U.S. Department of Education, Office of Technology Web site at **http://www.ed.gov/Technology/**, where you can find an alphabetical listing of State Technology Offices, Officers, and Technology Plans. You can also access an annotated list of Internet documents at the "Educational Standards and Curriculum Frameworks for Technology" Web site, **http://www.putwest.boces.org/StSu/Technology.html.** While not every state has published its standards on the Internet, the search-by-state section at this site will lead you to an appropriate online address where you can query your state directly.

North Carolina's model is an example of what is happening in some states and what can be expected to occur nationwide. Mastery of "computer proficiencies" will be a graduation requirement for all North Carolina high school students, beginning with the Class of 2000. These proficiencies, spelled out in the *North Carolina Standard Course of Study* (1992), are to be introduced "*collaboratively* by classroom teachers, media coordinators, and computer resource teachers" (3), beginning in kindergarten. The stated purpose of the K–12 curriculum is to prepare students to be "problem solvers, information seekers and users, and effective communicators . . . [who are] prepared for a technology-filled, twenty-first century world" (3). To achieve that purpose, state educators have developed a curricular framework based on three basic competency goals:

1. the understanding of "important issues of a technology-based society" and the exhibiting of "ethical behavior in the use of technology";

2. the "knowledge and skills in using computer technology"; and

3. the abilty to "use a variety of computer technologies to access, analyze, interpret, synthesize, apply and communicate information" (4–5).

While these are lofty goals that most teachers can applaud in theory, their accomplishment will take considerable commitment, given the present state of teacher training options, and the distance that education must go in order to catch up with the rest of society in functioning technologically.

We have to begin, certainly, with instructional uses in our own specialized fields. Most educators agree that an integrated use of technologies across the curriculum is the most effective way to make meaningful use of these new educational resources. One way the North Carolina model employs this approach is to suggest curriculum-relevant activities in connection with each skill required, suggesting that teachers develop similar activities appropriate for their students. For example, at the kindergarten level, children are expected to identify the physical components of a computer system and be able to locate letters and numbers on a keyboard. The "sample measures" suggested in the *Standard Course of Study* for this skill include coloring letters on a paper computer keyboard and choosing the correct picture of a "disk drive" or "monitor" after being given a verbal prompt. Of course, every teacher will find multiple ways to move beyond these basic suggestions. (Computer skills required at each grade level, along with the objectives that constitute the core curriculum, are outlined in Appendix C: Computers in the Language Arts Curriculum, Tables 1–4.)

But what do *teachers* need to know to meet this latest professional challenge? The North Carolina plan, *Computer Competencies for All Educators in North Carolina Public Schools,* requires that *all* educators be able to demonstrate a knowledge of the basic components of a computer system, including hardware and software applications; be able to perform basic functions, including loading, running, saving, and copying programs, and printing output; to know the instructional uses of computers as well as their effects on current issues in society, such as personal privacy, ethics, and copyright laws; and to be aware of their potential uses in such fields as robotics, artificial intelligence, and electronic research.

Beyond the information base and minimum skills development required for all educators, North Carolina content-area teachers are expected to be able to "design unit/lesson plans, evaluate and select appropriate computer courseware, plan effective utilization strategies, implement classroom computer activities, and evaluate the results" (6). And along with these core competencies for all content areas, North Carolina's certification in communication skills, aimed at English teachers, among others, specifies keeping up with the changing status of electronic technology, exhibiting familiarity with voice synthesizers, scanners, video cameras, desktop print formats, and almost anything else that is relevant in this rapidly changing field. To underline the importance of these goals, the North Carolina State Board of Education added a requirement in 1997 that three to five of the fifteen credits for teaching certificate renewal be in technology.

Beyond acquiring such knowledge and skills, we will have to change and enlarge our vision of classroom possibilties. Our teaching strategies, our classroom materials, our classrooms themselves will all reflect changes in the way we teach and learn. All teachers will soon be selecting and evaluating "courseware," using computers for tutorials and simulations, gathering information from data files, keeping student records in a computer file, and communicating by electronic network with teachers and learners around the world.

Aspiring teachers enrolled in education programs around the country will be asked to meet these new teacher-certification requirements, which means that teacher educators who are not now computer knowledgable must catch up in a hurry. And supervising teachers in the schools must do so as well, along with every other teacher who expects to be a part of tomorrow's schools.

Teaching at every level will reflect this new "age of information and communication." Students graduating from such a curriculum will enter colleges and universities with skills and expectations that are unimagined now, even by some of our most prestigious institutions. College and university professors will be meeting classrooms filled with computer-literate students who expect state-of-the-art teaching, and that includes electronic technologies. College classrooms, laboratories, and libraries will be places where students are increasingly guided in their own discovery of knowledge, and professors are partners and mentors in that search, rather than sources and arbiters of what constitutes knowledge or "cultural literacy." Across the curriculum, students and professors will be using computers for the most advanced kinds of research and communication. And the idea of literacy itself will continue to change as technology takes us into new worlds of voice and video transmission where text will take on wholly new forms.

Teacher Workshops

Teacher preparation is of prime importance to us in setting up our online literature programs. Much of this preparation has consisted of onsite meetings during which we discuss ways to use literature in the classroom as well as how to do computer networking with confidence. With a few dedicated people and a little planning, an onsite workshop can be the best way to begin. Research shows that the most effective training is done where teachers work in their own building, on their own equipment, to meet their own needs. State technology planners in cooperation with Bell South Corporation and the Southern Regional Education Board (SREB) also conclude that

> Teachers must not only know how to use various technologies, but also must have a clear understanding of how technology changes the learning process. Staff development should be used to help teachers develop teaching strategies and to explore the impact technology will have on their teaching methods. (Jones 12)

The SREB study is a helpful guide in planning staff development workshops, as are two other books on staff development, both from Scholastic, Inc.: *Creating a Technology Staff Development Program: An Administrator's Sourcebook for Redefining Teaching and Learning,* by Gerald Bailey and Dan Lumley; and *101 Activities for Creating Effective Technology Staff Development Programs,* by Gerald Bailey and Gwen Bailey.

Ongoing, onsite training in integrating technology into the curriculum is the key to successful curriculum change and to professional development. A workshop is a good start, but it is not enough. For this major shift in pedagogy, what is needed is cooperative learning in every classroom where peer mentors, master teachers, and onsite media and curriculum advisors can make this quantum leap together. And with the help of networks, schools can accelerate this process, bringing the world to their own classrooms, however remotely located. When funding does become available to plan a full-scale workshop or institute, we recommend a community-building structure in which teachers and media specialists can spend extended time together, as readers as well as teachers.

With funding from the North Carolina Humanities Council, we were fortunate enough to be able to call some teachers away from their classrooms for a week-long institute in an idyllic setting, at the North Carolina Center for the Advancement of Teaching. For the twenty-five teachers gathered there, we developed five days of sessions based on the needs that project participants had voiced to us over the years. Because teachers told us they needed both theory and practice, we divided each day into two major components: (1) theory about the use of literature in the classroom and (2) practice using an electronic communications network. We gave participants numerous articles on both of these subjects and sent them two paperback books to read beforehand: *Grand Conversations: Literature Groups in Action,* by Ralph Peterson and Maryann Eeds, and Cynthia DeFelice's *Weasel,* a historical fiction novel for middle-grade readers. We wanted the teachers to have *Grand Conversations* as common background information they could build upon as they attended sessions during the conference—sessions that addressed ways to get students talking in meaningful ways about books. And we wanted them to have an opportunity to practice what they were hearing by participating in small-group discussions of *Weasel.*

In our literature sessions, we talked about creating a literate community in the classroom, how to guide discussion groups, reader-response theory, using literature in the content areas, and using literature to teach writing. Several speakers put together text sets of books to show participants how to use literature in thematic teaching. We had book talk sessions in an effort to familiarize the teachers with the latest and best children's books available, and we set up a lending library so that they could borrow and read books during their free time. Storytellers and authors filled the evenings with stories and talk about literature.

A keynote speech on "Visions for Learning" by Margaret Gayle, co-author with Marvin Cetron of *Educational Renaissance,* helped push our thinking to new frontiers and fortified us in our determination to use this new technology meaningfully in our teaching. To aid us, we were able to schedule use of a computer lab and have two computer experts conduct the hands-on sessions. Half of each day was given over to explanations of the technology and actual practice using the network. Before the conference ended, participants paired with each other to develop plans for an online reading project to be implemented during that school year. A significant aspect of this workshop, we believe, was that the teachers themselves designed each project with their own and their students' needs in mind.

By coming together for this brief time, away from the demands of the teaching day, our participants were able to immerse themselves in talk about books and how to use them in the classroom. They were able to experience what it means to be surrounded with literature in a community of readers and writers and to share their insights with one another. They left with the resolve to facilitate these same experiences for their students.

It is important to keep in mind that even though you may not have the luxury of taking a full week away from school for inservice training, more than an afternoon workshop will be needed to ensure success in a project of this nature. It is important for you and the other teachers involved to become familiar with the technology and to practice with it before the students actually become involved. If you have a computer at home or available to you after school hours where you can practice, you can make more rapid gains. It is also important to learn as much as you can about using literature in the classroom. Brainstorm with teachers in your building; start teacher book discussion groups and have sessions at least once a month; bring in local authors and other outside speakers for workshop sessions. Be creative and be persistent. Teachers working together with other teachers provide the key to effective change.

Professional Development Opportunities

Opportunities abound for learning how to use technology in the classroom. For example, Tom Snyder Productions offers onsite workshops for teachers and teacher trainers as well as public seminars on *Great Teaching With Technology* at various sites around the country. The company also offers professional development materials, including *Great Teaching in the One Computer Classroom* by David Dockterman and *Teaching with the Internet: Lessons from the Classroom*. For more information you can visit Tom Snyder Productions Web site at **http://www.teachtsp.com.**

A number of individual consultants specialize in curriculum-related training. LitTech Associates, for example, provides workshops on the use of technology in the English classroom, with emphasis on fostering book discussions among students. Sessions are customized to meet the needs of individual schools. Contact LitTech Associates at **saccardi@soho.ios.com** or **mjody@wcu.campus.mci.net**.

Classroom Connect publishes *Net Seminar,* a do-it-yourself kit for technology trainers, and offers regional conferences for technology training through its "Internet Academy." These regional conferences promise eight days of preconference workshops, hands-on labs, and subject-specific sessions. The Web site for further information is **http://www.classroom.net**.

The International Society for Technology (ISTE), which sponsors the "ISTE Leadership Academy," provides training at conferences, in special workshops, in schools, and at home. Contact ISTE for more information at **http://www.iste.org**.

An increasing number of colleges and universities offer distance learning courses on technology in the classroom. For example, Indiana University offers courses on "Teaching with the Internet Across the Curriculum" and "The Online Classroom." Information about other distance learning opportunities is also available from the Indiana University distance learning page at **http://www.indiana.edu/~eric_rec/disted/menu.html**.

The Heritage Institute, a provider of continuing education for K–12 educators, offers graduate course credit through Antioch University for a number of online courses such as "Using the Computer to Enhance Your Classroom Curriculum." (Contact The Heritage Institute, 2802 E. Madison Ave., Suite 187, Seattle, WA 98112; **mail@hol.edu**.) Arizona State University offers an online course, "Computers in Education," designed to prepare teachers to use technology in the classroom (see **http://www.asu.cdu/xed/**). The University of Oregon, in conjunction with the International Society for Technology in Education (ISTE) offers an introductory course called "Internet for Educators." A course description can be found at **http://www.iste.org/profdev/de/CourseDescriptions.html**.

A search of the Internet will identify dozens of other appropriate online courses for professional development. New Promise, an index of online college courses (**http://www.newpromise.com**), is only one of several comprehensive listings online.

In addition to the opportunities for learning provided by professional organizations, software publishers, and schools and colleges, the computer industry itself has invested a great deal of money and interest in providing training for educators. IBM (**http://www.IBM.com**) and Apple (**http://www.apple.com**) both have education divisions you can contact for assistance and information about training opportunities. One of the major training sites that IBM funds is the comprehensive Institute for Academic Technology at Research Triangle, North Carolina, in cooperation with the University of North Carolina at Chapel Hill.

Microsoft and the Global SchoolNet Foundation have collaborated in expanding the Global Schoolhouse Web site to include opportunities for professional development (**http://www.gsh.org/**), while Compaq Computer Corporation sponsors a Teacher Development Grants program in cooperation with Scholastic's "Electronic Learning in Your Classroom" (the Web site is **http://scholastic.com/Instructor**).

Getting acquainted with some of the major organizations directly interested in technology and education is a good way to pursue professional development on your own. For a sense of what is happening on a grand scale try the National Educational Computing Conference (NECC), held yearly, and sponsored by a coalition of major societies for computer education, such as EDUCAUSE, a nonprofit consortium of colleges, universities, and corporate affiliates; the Association for Educational Communication and Technology (AECT); and the International Society for Technology in Education (ISTE), another nonprofit organization and a source of materials for teachers. ISTE publishes a newsletter for members called *Update,* as well as several journals, including *Technology and Learning* and *Journal of Computing in Teacher Education.* (Copies of proceedings from the NECC conferences can be ordered from ISTE.)

EDUCAUSE, a forum for exchange of ideas on issues relating to computing in higher education, publishes *Educom Review.* The Association for Supervision and Curriculum Development (ASCD) supports the Education and Technology Resources Center and publishes *Curriculum/Technology Quarterly.* Other excellent professional journals include *Electronic Learning, T.H.E. (Technological Horizons in Education) Journal,* and *Syllabus.*

You don't have far to look for a guide to everything-about-computers, including networking. Books devoted to the subject multiply almost daily, it seems. Selectivity can lead to any level or style of explanation, from primary to techno-babble. *The Internet Guide for English Language Teachers* by Dave Sperling is a good beginner's book, followed by the more detailed *Teacher's Complete and Easy Guide to the Internet,* by Ann Heide and Linda Stilborne. *The Book Lover's Guide to the Internet* by Evan Morris is another careful introduction to the Internet that will give you a good idea of just how much book-related material is out there on the Net.

Administrative and Technical Support

Even the most willing teachers need technical support and administrative backing to put an electronic reading program in place. Administrators will need to be proactive, seeking financial support, approving necessary changes in schedule and classrooms, making a computer specialist's time available, committing funds, and, best of all, taking part in book discussions themselves.

If you are a novice, and if you have a media specialist in your school, make arrangements to work with this person before or after school or during a prep period. While it might seem an unfair imposition on his or her time, it will save time in the long run as you become proficient enough to work on your own. If your school does not have its own computer specialist, perhaps there is one in the district with whom you can work. As Betty Bankhead writes, "Efficient management of technology is essential to maintaining your other responsibilities, your credibility, and your sanity" (49).

Using computers in the study of literature is not only a means of integrating computer skills into classroom learning, but also a way of keeping technology in its proper perspective. Only by exploring the possibilities ourselves will we truly know what the computer can and cannot do for our profession. Otherwise, those who think they know will surely direct those who ought to know.

Books on Computer

I think that talking to an author over the computer is totally space age! It's really cool.

—Sami, a seventh grader

When we first wrote *Computer Conversations,* we (and others) were calling books that were available online for reading or downloading "digital," or "digital electronic media." We distinguished those from interactive electronic books on CD-ROM, particularly the ones for children, where birds took flight and dogs barked at the click of a mouse. Then there was "hypertext fiction"—a new creation for older students that came in the form of an interactive narrative. Now the word "digital" seems to be passé, "electronic" is the term of choice, and earlier distinctions are variations on a much larger theme. We still try to keep these few categories for clarity.

Electronic Books

An electronic book is one that provides not only text and pictures, if there are any, on the screen, but also sound and graphics that encourage the reader to become more involved. A reader can ask to have an unfamiliar word repeated or defined, see illustrations come to life, and engage in supplemental reading and writing activities. Electronic books can bring the reader additional materials to peruse, maps or copies of original documents, for example, to enrich or clarify a subject. These books are appearing at a prolific rate, the field is highly competitive, and companies vie with one another to produce more sophisticated animation and graphics and greater opportunities for users to interact meaningfully with text. The brief sampling that follows will give some hint of the breadth of possibilities these high-tech books afford. While there are hundreds of enticing CD-ROMs now on the market, only those that are truly "books" are included here.

While some electronic books are available on floppy disk, most are on CD-ROM, and a computer must be equipped with a CD-ROM drive in order to read them. Grolier pioneered CD-ROM technology several years ago with its *Multimedia Encyclopedia,* and that was just the beginning of wonderful multimedia reference materials to come. Not only has Grolier continued to update its encyclopedia, having recently introduced its 1998 *Grolier Multimedia Encyclopedia,* but other companies have entered the reference market as well. There is something for every age group. DK Publishing's *My First Dictionary* demonstrates for children as young as three the meanings of words, provides synonyms, and much more. The *Bookman Merriam-Webster Collegiate Dictionary, Speaking Edition,* by Franklin Electronic Publishers, includes the entire dictionary plus thousands of pronunciations, a thesaurus and grammar guide, spelling corrections, and a subject feature. Microsoft's *Encarta '98 Encyclopedia Deluxe Edition* is a comprehensive source of reference information enabling users to browse through more than 32,000 articles, 3,500 new entries and articles updated in 1998. CD-ROM products like these make information come alive for students and gives them such varied experiences as witnessing an erupting volcano, watching a heart beat, or traveling the globe in search of information for their nonfiction writing.

Broderbund Software Company has published a series of electronic picture books, marketed for preschool through about sixth grade, called "Living Books." Among the titles now available are *Arthur's Teacher Trouble, Arthur's Birthday,* and *Arthur's Reading Race* by Marc Brown; *New Kid on the Block,* by Jack Prelutsky; *Grandma and Me* and *Little Monster at*

School, by Mercer Mayer; *Harry and the Haunted House* and *The Tortoise and the Hare* (retold) by Mark Schlichting; *Dr. Seuss's ABC, Green Eggs and Ham,* and *The Cat in the Hat* by Dr. Seuss; *Stellaluna* by Janelle Cannon; and *Sheila Rae, the Brave,* by Kevin Henkes. When using these electronic books, students can choose the "Read to Me" mode, in which the story is read aloud in either English or Spanish (one of the books even has a text in Japanese) while words are highlighted. If they want a word repeated or defined, students can click the mouse on it. In the "Let Me Play" mode, students can move through the different pages at their leisure, listening as the story is read aloud, and clicking the mouse on various graphics which then come to life with different sounds and animation. Some books offer the opportunity for increased involvement, for example, choosing levels of play or participating in quizzes. While certainly making reading a fun activity, these electronic books encourage young children to do what all good readers do—interact with the text. The animation helps students focus on different aspects of the illustrations and, in some cases, even gets them inside characters' minds to uncover thoughts and motivations. Broderbund also publishes accompanying materials that provide teachers with many whole language classroom applications.

The National Geographic Society publishes a CD-ROM library that explores science and nature in twenty-three books on five CD-ROMs. The series is directed at kindergarten through third-grade students and is specifically designed for Macintosh computers. The five different titles, each consisting of four or five books, are *A World of Animals, Our Earth, The Human Body, A World of Plants,* and *Animals and How They Grow.* Children using these electronic books can slow down the narration, pause to have words defined, and hear words translated into Spanish. All or portions of the text can be heard read aloud in English or Spanish. Students can select objects in the photographs, and the computer will produce sound effects, display name labels, and pronounce the names. Activity sheets can be printed out to accompany the reading.

National Geographic also offers 108 years of its magazine on CD-ROM. Users can scan for articles, photographs, maps, and more, by date, issue, topic, key words, or title. There are also links to a Web site available exclusively for the CD-ROM user.

The "First Adventures Bookshelf' from Computer Curriculum Corporation contains twenty-two books, sixteen in English and six in Spanish, for children in grades 1 and 2. These electronic books, written by well-known authors, provide a multitude of interactive opportunities that support reading, writing, listening, and speaking. There is a "storyteller" mode that allows children to listen to the stories. Or, if they prefer, they can chose a "read-along" option. A glossary screen comes into view when a child clicks on a highlighted word. Through an online notepad feature, children can write responses to the stories they read and record their voices. Teachers may also customize stories for individual children. There are pre- and postreading comprehension activities and assessment tools.

Scholastic, Inc., has developed a series of seventy-two electronic books for K–2 students called "Wiggleworks," available in English and Spanish. There are three stages, each containing twenty-four books. Each stage is quite expensive ($1,750 at this writing) but does contain a variety of materials, among which are six copies of each of the twenty-four books, a CD-ROM or floppy disk version (depending on your system), an audiocassette for each book, and a teaching guide.

The animation in these books is not as sophisticated as that in the "Living Books" series, but teacher and students have many more opportunities for interaction. The reading component works much the way the "Living Books" series does. Children can have a book read to them, can highlight individual words, and see the text highlighted word by word or line by line. In addition, they have opportunities to interact in writing with the text. Students can keep a notebook of special words from the text that they want to remember, write their own responses to a book, illustrate on screen, or innovate from the text by writing their own versions of the story. Students can even record their own reading of the original text or their own writing. The computer will play a voice-synthesized reading of their own writing back to them, helping emerging writers to see where they might have left out words or notice words whose spelling is so far from conventional as to render them incomprehensible.

Teachers, too, can interact with the books. They can greet individual students as they log on to the system, give specific instructions such as, "collect all the animal words in this story," ask questions, and more. Teachers can also ask students to play with words on an electronic letter magnet board, much the way Reading Recovery teachers use magnetized letters to help their students build words. "Wiggleworks" is truly a system that incorporates reading, writing, speaking, and listening in an attractive, albeit expensive, package.

One of the advantages of the "Discis Books" program from Discis Knowledge Research, is that students from grades 1–5 can select a word in any of the many stories available and hear it in another language choice such as Spanish, French, and Cantonese. Folktales and other children's books are included.

Scholastic also has an electronic book series called "Smartbooks." Thus far there is a packet that includes six copies of the trade book, a teaching guide, and CD-ROM for each of the following titles: *If Your Name Was Changed at Ellis Island, Malcolm X: By Any Means Necessary, Favorite Greek Myths,* and *Exploring the Titanic.*

Traditional or folk literature is one of the most important genres we can offer our students, and wonderful tales are available as electronic books. Davidson's "Story Club" is a multimedia language development system for preschool through sixth grade. Folktales from around the world are read using human voices. The program includes a multimedia photo dictionary. There are cooperative learning activities for oral and written language development. Students can explore within the tales as well as write, illustrate, and record their own original stories. Hartley's "Stories to Grow On" for preschool through third grade includes several favorite folktales. Children can read along, interact with the text, and even create their own stories. The Milliken Publishing Company's "Interactive Learning Series" includes classic children's tales read in a human voice with words underlined to help children follow the text. Students can write their own stories and color the pictures on the screen. An original music score enhances each of the many traditional tales available from Queue's "Favorite Fairy Tales," a program suitable for primary grade students.

The "Reading Magic Library" series, intended for grades K–2, includes interactive electronic books for Macintosh and Windows put out by Tom Snyder Productions. The five stories now available can be used with three modes—Read, Write, and Record—and are available on two different reading levels: "Standard" and "Early Reader." The "Early Reader" level uses language that is easier for emergent readers. Individuals or groups of children can work with the text. At various points in the story, users must decide which way the story will proceed. The computer selects the person who must make the choice. Using the "Read" mode, teachers can hide words that appear in the story, substituting the number that corresponds to the number of letters in the missing word. While doing this Cloze practice activity, users can uncover the hidden words by hitting the space bar for each letter. Using the "Write" mode, students can retell the story to accompany graphics that appear on the screen, and they can print their story. In the "Record" mode, children (or the teacher) can record and save their own readings.

Some of the wildly popular "Magic School Bus" books are now available on CD-ROM from Microsoft. Each story comes with games, facts, and jokes, and an interactive experiment related to the aspect of science explored in the book.

For older students, an interactive version of Edgar Allan Poe's chilling short story "The Tell-Tale Heart" is available on CD-ROM from Discis Knowledge Research. Students can listen to the text read without interruption, hear two different narrators, and view eighteen color drawings. They can have words defined, hear pronunciations, identify parts of speech, and have access to questions and commentary. Westwind Media has an unabridged electronic version of Poe's "The Fall of the House of Usher." The text is presented in seventy-two scenes with animated illustrations and different voices for the narrator and characters. Students can also access critical analysis and biographical information about the author and test their knowledge of the story by playing a game. For readers in grades 7–12, the BookWorm Library Series CD-ROM for Macintosh and Windows contains fourteen titles, including several of Shakespeare's plays and *Little Women*. Students can customize each book, creating their own multimedia edition of the work. Also for older readers, there is a comprehensive look at the poetry of Robert Frost entitled *Robert Frost: Poetry, Life, Legacy*, a CD-ROM made available by Henry Holt. This CD-ROM contains the complete text of all of Frost's poems, videos of his life, critical essays, and much more. Students can hear Frost himself read some of his poetry, and keep their own electronic notebook of favorite poems and other information.

Readers of the electronic age can also turn to "Twain's World," a multimedia CD-ROM from Bureau Development, Inc., that contains the complete works of Mark Twain as well as photographs, narration, biography, and animation. Middle school students will also enjoy Southern Star Interactive's *The Adventures of Tom Sawyer.* This CD-ROM for Windows and Macintosh contains the complete text of the novel, a biography of the author, a narrated slide show entitled "Mississippi River Life," and comprehension games. Students can also combine text and pictures to create their own slide show.

Even textbooks are appearing as electronic books on CD-ROM. *The African American Experience* from Computerized Educational Resources tells the story of African Americans, beginning on the African continent, for students from the sixth grade on up. Students can move back and forth throughout the ten units of the text, access biographical sketches, historical documents, and galleries of musicians, writers, artists, and scientists. *The American Indian: A Multimedia Encyclopedia* is a comprehensive program from Facts on File. It focuses on more than 150 Native American tribes in the United States and Canada and contains four complete texts. In the main menu alone, students can access history, biography, tribes, legends, photos, maps, drawings, sounds, documents, tribe locations, and museums. Documents from the National Archives and rare maps are also available in this text for high school and college students.

A software guide or the shelves of your local software store will reveal just how fast the body of electronic books is growing.

Hypertext Fiction

One of the most intriguing developments in literature and technology is the "hypertext novel." While any computer game whiz will find these works at least familiar looking, the reader of *novels,* as that term is generally understood, will have to do more than a double-take. In fact, the number of "takes," so to speak, is what hypertext is all about.

As Howard Holden explains (see Appendix D), "Hypertext is the linking of separate but related documents" in a way somewhat like that of annotated footnotes, which contain material "not essential to the text, but [which] may direct the reader's attention to pertinent sources and other information."

Reading hypertext fiction is an associative process, unlike the linear act of reading a conventional text, in which the reader processes pages sequentially. Instead, the reader selects unnumbered hypertext "pages" on the screen, sometimes randomly, sometimes by choosing one pathway or another, by selecting from options within the text. Each "reading" differs from a previous sequencing of blocks of text.

Sound confusing? Maybe. But as Patti Johnson, the Western Carolina University MicroNet Wizard of Oz, likes to say, "It's easier done than said." Well-known writer Robert Coover, who teaches a course on writing hyperfiction at Brown University, has commented on the phenomenon in a useful article for the *New York Times Book Review*. Speaking of *Victory Garden*, a hypertext novel by Stuart Moulthrop, Coover writes:

> [I]n spite of all the overt play . . . there is really only one story here, as whole and singular—ultimately linear, even chronological—as that of any ordinary print novel—the only difference being that the reader moves about in the story as though trying to remember it, the narrative having lost its temporality by slipping whole into the past, becoming there a kind of obscure geography to be explored. (10)

The pioneer publisher of serious hypertext fiction, Eastgate Systems, has created its own software, Storyspace, to run these "books" on either Windows or Macintosh. In addition to *Victory Garden,* the novel reviewed by Robert Coover, their titles include, among others, one of the earliest, *Afternoon, A Story,* and one of the most recent, *Twilight, A Symphony,* both by Michael Joyce. "Reading" hypertext fiction is to experience a wholly new kind of adventure in perception. For a look at these and other intriguing works, examine Eastgate's Web site at **http://www.eastgate.com**. For more about hypertext fiction, you can read an online journal such as *Hyperizons: The Hypertext Fiction Homepage* (**http://www.duke.edu/~mshumate/hyperfic.html**). Links from this site will take you to another informative piece, "Tracing the Growth of a New Literature," by Michael Shumate, an exceptionally rich description of the past, present, and future of this new medium. This article can also be accessed directly at **http://www.december.com/cmc/mag/1996/dec/shumate.html**.

To sample old familiar literature as seen through the eyes of hypertext, you might turn to Jane Austen's *Pride and Prejudice* for another concept of ways that hypertext can be used in the study of literature (**http://uts.cc.utexas.edu/~churchh/pridprej.html**). Links in this document take you to every corner of the novel and its relation to the author's life and work.

The deluge of information available through this new medium challenges old assumptions about where and how literary learning can or should take place.

Online Bookstores

For teachers of the language arts eager to know about the latest books and bring them to their students, bookstores online are a great boon. Now it is possible to read about books as or even before they are published, to read reviews of these books, to learn about their authors, and to order them instantly online, often at a good discount. The ability to search these online bookstores' inventory by title, author, and subject enables teachers to put together bibliographies of books on any subject they wish to teach

and is an enormous time-saver. It also enlarges the possibilities for information since we are not limited to the holdings of our local public or school libraries. Here are a few of our favorite online bookstore sites:

Amazon.com
http://www.amazon.com

Far and away our favorite, this online bookstore contains over two million titles, most available for purchase at a 10 to 40 percent discount. Since it is possible to search these titles by author and/or subject, Amazon also provides a quick and easy way to obtain bibliographies of books on a variety of topics taught in the classroom. There are annotations, book reviews, interviews with authors, contests, and the possibility of adding reviews for books that teachers and students have read. Amazon editors, if asked to do so, will notify subscribers via e-mail about the latest books on a requested subject or by a specific author.

CIBON (Comprehensive Independent Booksellers
Online Network)
http://www.bookweb.org/bookstores/

Browse a list of over 4,500 booksellers, complete with URLs, e-mail addresses, and descriptions. Easily track down bookstores in your corner of the world.

Computer Literacy (Bookshops + Online)
http://www.clbooks.com/

This Web site contains a wealth of information on computer books, magazines, hardware, and much more.

Powell's Books
http://www.powells.portland.or.us/

Over a million new and used books are available at this site. Readers can search the site by title, author, and subject. There is a rare books section, a used books section, and one for out-of-print books.

Printers Inc. Bookstore
http://www.pibooks.com/index.html

At this site Web readers can order books online, search for titles, see conversations with authors, obtain lists of monthly bestsellers, and more.

Stiltjack Books, Limited
http://www.cityscape.co.uk/users/ds36/

This is a British bookshop specializing in book search services. They have a small stock of modern books.

Online Libraries

How many times have we needed to go to the library to do research and been unable to get there? Or wanted to use the library after hours? Since we discovered that not only our local libraries but also the Library of Congress and many university libraries throughout the world are available to us twenty-four hours a day, seven days a week on the Internet, our lives have become much easier. Now we can see what holdings our local library has on a particular subject, determine whether a particular book we would like is actually on the shelves, and even reserve it until we can pick it up in person. If the local library does not have the book we want, we can see what other libraries in the state hold it. And we can do all this without ever leaving our computer screens at home! For more extensive research, the Library of Congress and other major libraries are there on the Internet to serve us. The Library of Congress catalogs are searchable using a word search, a browse search, a command search, or an experimental search system. Each method is described at the Library's site: **http://lcweb.loc.gov/homepage/online.html**. The site also lists the library's tools for blind and physically handicapped persons, a Vietnam War database, and a wealth of additional information.

To find out whether your local library is online, call and ask, or look it up using one of the many search engines (see Chapter 7) available on the Web. Your local library may also provide a training course for those interested in using the Web and/or allow patrons to access the Web at computer terminals in the library. Now that we have gotten hooked on library searches on the Web, we wonder how we ever managed without this time-saving service!

Books Online

A small library of books, from Dante to Stephen King, is already online as electronic texts that you can transport from their source to your own personal computer. Some are in plain text, others in hypertext. As Howard Holden points out in "Turning the Page: Reading in the DEM," the advent of the printing press gave a sense of "permanence" to "knowledge" and "truth" in books. But, he continues, "Peering into a new millennium we know . . . [while] knowledge and books have revolutionized the world over and over . . . , only recently have books themselves begun to be revolutionized" (2). And that transformation may in fact have repercussions of unexpected dimensions on the durability of an authoritative statement, which may now endure only until the next electronic message supercedes it.

In re-examining our concept of books and reading, it is worth considering Holden's cautionary statement:

> [T]he printing press gave us something far more valuable than information. It gave us reading. Slow, quiet, introspective, character-building reading. The DEM [digital electronic media] has made information available on the "information highway" at nearly the speed of light, which can certainly enhance our knowledge; but maybe we should rebuild some back roads ("Turning" 20).

Project Gutenberg—appropriately named—is an example of what an electronic library looks like. When Michael Hart, working on a mainframe computer at the University of Illinois in 1971, was given a one hundred million dollar opportunity to do something significant with computers, he decided to put the great books on it for everyone to use. The first e-texts he presented were the Declaration of Independence and the U.S. Constitution, including the Bill of Rights, followed by Shakespeare and the original Gutenberg's first choice, the Bible. Project Gutenberg, which calls itself the

"Mother of All E-Text Archives," now lists more than a thousand books available on the Web. By the year 2001, the Gutenburg Project visualizes having 10,000 e-texts in distribution. By then, project planners assure us, computers of the era will easily hold a library of that size, and they predict an audience of 100 million computers, with a user audience much greater than that. Thus their "conservative" estimate of the potential number of e-texts to be distributed by the year 2001 is 10,000 e-texts to 100 million users, a total distribution of one trillion e-texts.

Project Gutenberg argues that the value of this project is based on making texts cheap and easy to use, available no matter how many people "check them out," and never out of circulation for rebinding, never lost, never stolen. In an age of electronic libraries, they tell us librarians will be consultants and libraries will fit in the palm of your hand. The cost of the whole library is estimated at about one cent per book.

Online Books (**http://www.cs.cmu.edu/books.html**) has indexed more than 5,000 titles available online, many of which can be downloaded or printed free. This Web site also lists many other sites that specialize in searching for or distributing e-texts. For example, one such site (**http://www.writersworld.net/banned/Banned_Books.html**) specializes in listing "banned books." Of course, the site itself has been the object of censorship attempts, and is "banned" by NetNanny software, a popular screening device. As we know, even stories like "Little Red Riding Hood" are on at least someone's banned list (yes, it's on this list too). While caution is advised for the classroom, for a study of censorship and the books that have been the object of it, this site is significant.

Another caution: not all texts available electronically are in the public domain. Use of any electronic text should be governed by the same cautionary "fair use" policies that apply to classroom use of printed works of literature.

For those whose computers lack storage capacity to receive lengthy texts, a list of electronic texts currently available on IBM and Macintosh floppy disks can be obtained from sources like B&R Samizdat Express (**http://www.samizdat.com**). This *Please Copy This Disk* collection has public domain electronic texts in American and English literature, like *The Last of the Mohicans* and *Dr. Jekyll and Mr.Hyde,* and children's literature, such as *The Secret Garden* and *At the Back of the North Wind.* Spectrum is another potential source of e-texts on floppy disk. Their catalog is available by e-mail from **specpress@earthlink.net**.

The publication of Stephen King's short story "Umney's Last Case" on the Internet, *before* it was made available in the hardcover collection *Nightmares and Dreamscapes,* was an early indication of just how fast the publishing world is changing. In response to this shift to electronic formats, a number of centers like the Center for Electronic Texts in the Humanities, a joint project of Princeton and Rutgers Universities funded by the National Endowment for the Humanities, are cataloging machine-readable texts, preparing texts for distribution on computer networks, and developing summer training institutes for teachers and scholars in the humanities.

From use in reading-for-pleasure projects to in-depth exploration of literature, electronic texts are making their way into English classrooms in ever-increasing numbers. Electronic books, hypertext fiction, and online libraries can be exciting adjuncts to discussions of printed texts, while their interactive nature can make them a logical bridge to a growing community of readers who use electronic networks for book talk—no matter what format has brought them the book.

Networks and Conversations Online

6

In the BookRead project, I experimented with cooperative learning as I had never done before, I used the vast capabilities of word processing as I had never done before, and I challenged and observed my students immersing themselves in literature as I had never done before.

—Mike DeVito, teacher

The Internet is a network of networks, the largest computer network in the world, connecting millions of people and linking every continent. It all began in 1969 with DARPANET, a Defense Department initiative that allowed computers to communicate with each other over telephone lines. By the early 1980s the National Science Foundation had joined with the Department of Defense to expand the network, allowing a sharing of information among government and university researchers. Now the number of computer connections, from giant corporations to individual users, is in the many millions and multiplying daily. Nationwide access for all schools in every community will certainly be achieved before the year 2000 as the information highway is completed.

Getting Started

Connecting to the Internet usually means either direct access through your school or business, or a dial-up account with an Internet service provider. Most schools have or soon will have a dedicated telephone line that is permanently connected to the Internet. At home, you will be dialing (through the modem, built into or attached to your computer) a telephone number provided by your Internet service provider. You might choose to subscribe to a major online service such as America Online or Prodigy or connect through a major telephone company service such as AT&T or MCI, a national service provider like Netcom, or one of hundreds of regional independent service providers. Your local library or yellow pages can help you locate one.

What Happens on a Network

While the Internet is one large entity, what happens there is multifaceted. You will probably first discover e-mail (electronic mail), the World Wide Web (see Chapter 7 for a full discussion), mailing LISTS, and USENET (Internet discussion groups), the most commonly employed functions known to most users of the Internet. You'll discover ways to find library holdings and other sources of information called *databases* using search tools with intriguing names like Gopher, Wais, and Archie, and you'll bring whole documents into your own computer by means of file transfer protocol (FTP). Through the Internet, users can search for and retrieve information from electronic "card catalogues" and information repositories worldwide. Chat, another mode of electronic communication available on the Internet, makes simultaneous "conversation" possible as users type messages to each other in real time. Even audio and video conferencing are available on the Net, while still more exotic applications appear on the horizon. The Internet is a growing realm of possibility where learning can happen in innumerable ways, from a project as simple as a "key pals" (electronic pen pals) exchange to an adventure in space via virtual reality.

Communicating

E-mail puts a message in a "mailbox" at an individual address on the network, anywhere in the world. You can send a message at any time of the day (or night, depending on your access), and retrieve one from another sender at any time as well—simply by logging in (connecting to the network) and checking your mailbox. The ease of access to this greatly expanded neighborhood is staggering at first, even to adults. Sending your first message to someone in Australia or Japan and getting a response, sometimes on the same day, can be an exciting moment even for sophisticates. Educators increasingly list global awareness and cultural sensitivity among the appropriate objectives of classroom e-mail connections. This world view is a common one in cyberspace, where visas are not required.

Besides writing to individuals through e-mail, you can join one of thousands of groups of like-minded persons by subscribing to an Internet discussion group. Electronic mailing lists allow you to exchange e-mail with an entire group of people subscribed to the same list. Newsgroups, another form of discussion group similar to lists, post messages for each other in spaces reserved for particular interest groups. These groups—currently about 20,000 of them—are arranged in categories, indicated by the first three letters in the address, for example, "rec" for recreational activities and hobbies. You could be getting messages by e-mail from AMLIT-L, a mailing list for people interested in American literature, and messages in your newsreader from rec.arts.books, a much more general and less scholarly group. If you join a very active list or Newsgroup, be prepared to have your mailbox or newsreader flooded with messages. And when you subscribe, be sure to copy and save the instructions that will be sent to you on how to "unsubscribe" as well! Dave Sperling's book *The Internet Guide: For English Language Teachers* is a clear and concise guide to using the Internet. Another fine book is *The Teacher's Guide to the Internet,* by Ann Heide and Linda Stilborne.

Going Online

Conducting a project such as BookRead, described in Chapter 1, could prove to be a practical place for some teachers to start, while for others having their classes join a project such as those offered by America Online or Prodigy might be the best way to begin.

Conducting a regular literature class online is another attractive possibility. In the examples that follow we describe some of our own experiences with offering courses online. Like our account of the BookRead project, they are meant as prompts for your own ideas, adapted to your own circumstances. Whatever direction you take, we believe that the only place to begin is where you are, and the time to begin is now.

Samples from the Network

One of our early experiments in online teaching connected students on two very different kinds of university campuses—Teachers College of Columbia University, in New York City, and Western Carolina University, in Cullowhee, North Carolina. The course was taught on campus in New York as a regular classroom offering. At the same time, it was offered online for the students in North Carolina, using WCU MicroNet.

At their initial class meeting in North Carolina, students were met by their professor, given the course syllabus, shown how to access the network with their login names and passwords, assigned to reading groups, and given time for hands-on practice. When they next logged on, they were greeted by a "welcome" message from their instructor—now in New York. The greeting in their individual mailboxes was followed by the first assignment, based on a story assigned in the syllabus:

> E-mail message from the instructor: Welcome to your Micronet mailbox! You will be receiving mail messages all semester at this "address." Of course, you will be writing to others as well. To make sure that you have found this message, send your response to the first assignment, following the instructions below:

The assignment asked for a personal response to the story, to be sent by e-mail, with the identifying header "Personal Response," or "PR":

Assignment #1: Personal Response
Story: Kate Chopin, "The Story of an Hour"

Write a paragraph expressing your initial thoughts and feelings about the story. Send it by e-mail to the instructor and to your reading group.

Following the assignment was a short "tutorial," reinforcing what they had learned at the hands-on networking session:

Tutorial:

1. Quit reading your mail now by typing a "q," followed by a carriage return. You will be returned to the MicroNet main menu.

2. From the main menu, choose "mail."

3. From the mail menu, choose "send mail."

4. When asked for recipient, type:

   To: [story1, story 2, story3, etc.]
   Subject: PR: The Story of an Hour

5. When you have finished writing your message, type a period on a line by itself. Your message will be sent immediately.

The instructions were followed by a suggestion that they send mail messages to themselves first—by simply addressing e-mail to their own "user names"—to practice before writing the assignment.

Similar assignments followed, with tutorials for each new network function employed, such as class conferencing and creating a database. As the students were given additional assignments in reading the short story, they were also learning the networking skills necessary to complete them. After the first few weeks, only occasional technical guidance was necessary.

To achieve the ease and openness on a computer screen that is central to a reader-response classroom, we used online reading journals, small-group class discussion, and collaborative projects online, just as in the regular classroom. Students sent their initial responses to their reading groups of four or five, and later reacted to focus questions, trying out their ideas among their reading group by sending e-mail simultaneously to all members of the group and to the instructor.

For the instructor, reading the e-mail discussion was similar to moving around the classroom, entering in when it seemed appropriate, but the increased freedom of discussion was noticeable immediately. Even though students knew the instructor was looking in and they were being seen in print by their peers, they still seemed to open up more quickly than they ordinarily did in class. The privacy of a reading journal could be maintained as a personal file, if readers chose, but once they began writing to each other on screen, it seemed unlikely, judging from the content, that any but the most intimate thoughts were being held back!

As initial responses to the reading were shared more immediately, first in small-group settings and later in conference with the class as a whole, the self-consciousness of writing for an audience continued to dissipate. The semi-anonymity of the screen gave everyone equal voice. The shy became talkative; the talkative spoke less and more meaningfully; gender and racial barriers that too often mar free discussion in the classroom diminished or disappeared. Within the first few weeks, the online students were having the kind of discussion we work so long to achieve in a regular classroom.

It was obvious in advance that without a place and time to meet, the online class would need to have some kind of schedule in place of classroom time. Since the students were free to communicate twenty-four hours a day, seven days a week—a potential nightmare of confusion—the course was set up on a simple weekly schedule that was distributed with the syllabus. By midnight (it seemed an exotic time) of the day assigned, students were to have completed the day's task. The same held true for the instructor, so everyone could depend on a timely response, and the instructor could maintain some sort of order in her week as well. The course syllabus specified the text, reading assignments, due dates, and a set of basic weekly assignments, along with the network format for each message. The syllabus was online of course, for easy reference.

The schedule worked fairly well, once everyone realized they could do any of the assignments in *advance* of deadlines. Once we established that every assignment must have a standard message header (such as "PR" for "personal response"), assignments were easy to retrace. Many helpful class management tools now exist to aid in running a course online or a classroom on network, but these were days of experimentation. As a result, we learned that any teacher can create or customize simple management tools that are appropriate to the classroom or the course.

While the students read and responded to reading assignments, wrote to each other, and sent their individual thoughts and questions in e-mail messages to the instructor, she prepared a weekly equivalent of a classroom "lecture." The comments that seemed appropriate for the class on campus in New York had to be shrunk to fit a screen or two on the computer, a time-consuming challenge, but a useful reminder of just how much more we say than students need to hear, or can usefully absorb in one class meeting. While less was "said," the students online seemed to "listen" better and think more. The question of what it is that we really need to "teach" became much more than a theoretical one. The following sample of a "Lecture on Plot in One Screen" will illustrate:

> The reader of fiction learns very early that a story consists of a character or characters involved in significant action. The arrangement of that action is called *plot*. The *central action* of the plot, the most important movement or change that occurs in the story, may be mental, physical, emotional, even spiritual. A change of mind or a change of heart can be just as significant on the level of plot as a change of circumstance or behavior. Often at the heart of a story's plot is *conflict,* a problem. The dramatic revelation of this problem or the fictional resolution of the conflict is what makes *story* different from simple narration. A story must raise expectations, create suspense (sometimes called "intense expectancy"), arouse interest in what will happen next.

An equally brief assignment followed the "lecture":

> Beginning with these basics, let's look at Kate Chopin's story ["The Story of an Hour"] and attempt to identify the conflict. Opposing forces in a story may be two characters; but the antagonist may also be nature, society, fate, or the protagonist's own being. Start then with a focus question on *plot* as one way of approaching this story: Could the conflict raised by the story have been resolved in any way other than by Mrs. Mallard's death?

It was clear that much of what had ordinarily been said in class could be condensed, replaced when necessary by outside reading assignments, or addressed directly as questions came up. What the teacher *could* do more of online was respond directly to every student, guide the group by asking questions relevant to their own comments, applaud good reading, point to alternative readings, emphasize missed elements, summarize the patterns that had emerged from their responses, fill in gaps—in short, *teach* more and *inform* less. And the text of the students' comments remained in computer files, to respond to, not just in a few hours of face-to-face encounter, or in preprocessed papers, but on screen, whenever they were called up.

Critics on Call

One of the experimental features in this early experience that proved especially useful was a variation on the author-online element of BookRead, what we called the "critic-on-call," an outside expert who could comment on and answer questions about particular works or authors. It was rewarding to have a number of colleagues volunteer in response to an open request sent to members of the English department at Western Carolina University. Four brave pioneers came forward that first semester, on the promise that their involvement would be limited to one or two appearances online. Dr. Steve Eberly joined us for D. H. Lawrence, Dr. James Addison was our James Joyce commentator, Dr. Elizabeth Evans was our Flannery O'Connor expert, and Dr. Denise Heinze gave us her expertise on Toni Morrison. They provided the best kind of assistance not only to students, who benefited from the depth of the faculty members' own specialized knowledge, but to the instructor as well, thereby enriching the experience for all of us.

Obviously we can turn to experts online from around the world through the Internet, and in subsequent courses we have since done that as well. But "critics-on-call" who are experts from our own schools can enliven the discussion and enrich the learning and, at the same time, extend interest among the faculty in using technology for literary discussion and professional development. The resulting commonality of interest growing out of such teacher collaboration is a significant added benefit. No one feels too burdened by taking part on such a limited basis, and scheduling is easy, since the teacher can "visit" the class at any time or place that is convenient, from any computer connected to the network.

Student Collaboration

One of the remarkable benefits of offering the course in two places was the opportunity it gave students to share their perceptions of the course, as taught in two different ways. In fact, two students paired up via computer to compare notes on the way the course they were both taking was being taught in these very different settings. Their final paper, written collaboratively, concluded—not surprisingly—that both settings had value and should be combined. We agreed, and set about designing our next online course.

A graduate seminar that was ordinarily scheduled to meet twice a week instead met once a week in a regular class setting, then followed up with a second meeting online. In addition to completing their specific weekly assignments online, students could rehash what had happened in class and comment to each other, either as a group in the class conference, or privately by e-mail. They could also communicate with the instructor, of course, in the same ways between weekly class meetings.

In just one semester, seven students created a bibliography of nearly 150 entries, a compilation which they could all copy to a personal floppy disk for future use. In those fifteen weeks they wrote nearly three hundred messages, some of which kicked off freewheeling discussions that spilled over into the next week's class meeting or which followed up online what had begun in the classroom. The students then capped off the semester with a week-long, online, collaborative final examination, designed to be a simulation of the Master's Degree Written Comprehensive for which they were all preparing. A sample of that exam and the last wildly interesting exchange in response will provide a sense of what the course was like throughout:

I. *Identifications:* See how many you can answer of the following thirty identification questions. Compare scores. Ask your classmates to tell you the answers to the ones you don't know. Divide them up—four each—and write *good* one- or two-sentence answers for twenty-eight of them. Sign your individual contributions.

II. Write a concise, well-organized essay on any *two* of the following. You may divide up the task any way you see fit.

A. Some early character types in American literature include the frontiersman, the Yankee, and the cracker-barrel philosopher. Identify an American character *type* (male or female) to be found in twentieth-century American literature. Exemplify the type using examples from a convincing number of works.

B. The search for values in modern America has led to a number of literary explorations into existentialism. Decribe how at least three major works of the twentieth century express or examine the existential point of view.

C. The experience of African Americans has been expressed throughout American literature. Describe and illustrate the characteristics of that continuing subject/theme as it is found in American literature since World War I.

D. In an effort to convey the complexity of twentieth-century life, writers have experimented extensively with narrative point of view. Exemplify that reality by decribing at least three such stylistic experiments.

The responses during a week-long dialogue ranged from the hilarious to the astute:

from T__:

what is a cracker barrel philospher? never heard that term before. what exactly is the definition of existentialism? i think it is the belief that the individual is the most important aspect of life and that it does not matter what that individual does because we are going to die anyway. please, more help on this.

from MW__:

"Beloved" takes place earliest historically. The characters in the novel are adjusting to the relatively new "freedom" of African Americans approximately (!) fifteen years after slavery was abolished in the U.S. Morrison vividly describes how tenuous this freedom is; the characters are forever dealing with the hypocrisy in attitudes of the white community, certainly a recurring characteristic in A.A. literature . . .

Some messages were exercises in organization and leadership:

from K__:

If we do two essays together as a group, I think we should do one of the ones that T__ has answered, since we have done the existentialism one already, and he has already done C and D.

from M__:

Question C: In order to describe the theme of the experience of African Americans in literature since WW I, I will mention three of the novels that we read in common: Morrison's *Beloved,* Ellison's *Invisible Man,* and Faulkner's *Light in August.*

from T__:

ah, I thought of some for question "d." if we all picked two works on this and described them we would have a nice essay. no let's say three no two. gotta go before before somebody picks up the phone again. so long and stay in touch.

As the week's efforts continued, the group chatted in between bursts of work:

from T__:

hello my friends out in computerland. it's a chilly morning here at the farm and i'm glad we have central heat lest my fingers would be too cold until noon to write. on the id's: i can answer most of them—except 6, 7, 8, 18, and 30. since karen has picked two i shall pick #2 and #25 for mine. karen, i will tell you #28 soon as well. who can help me on mine?

from K__:

Okay guys and gals. I have put all of our IDs so far in one place for easy reference. Let me know if I have made any errors: [a compilation of thirty IDs followed.]

from MW__:

This conference-exam is the most fun I've had with any Exam I can remember. I feel like we are sitting around ripping our hair out together, which comforts me to no end . . . . I think we're doing fine, by the way.

from MK__:

Hello teammates. Sorry it took me so long to get back. Well, I have done an edit/compilation of the existentialism entries. Here it is for what it's worth. At least Dr. J. can still read everything in its entirety if she needs to: The existentialist philosophy coincides with modernism . . . . Like postmodernists, existentialists don't have much faith in society and concepts . . . . [A complete essay answer followed.]

Student evaluations of the course indicated they had not only learned a great deal about the literature, but also about writing more effectively and with greater ease. They had developed an unusually strong sense of camaraderie, having shared some profound ideas and strong emotional responses with each other in this unexpectedly intimate medium. They had learned how to disagree while respecting other opinions; they had begun to cooperate and help each other in a common learning experience, rather than competing for attention and grades. By the end of the semester they were reluctant to give up what had become an ongoing interaction with each other about books and ideas and the sense of community that had grown out of their shared experience. In their final messages, they wrote:

i have always hated goodbyes . . . . i have enjoyed this class immensely . . . . i have learned so much about computers and literature and about life (literature is a great help in sorting out ideas about life). it's been fun to see everyone's interactions. everybody contributed in their own special way. i like diversity and that's what the main strength of the class was (among other things). the class made me realize how much and how important literature is to me. . . . if you become writers, look me up down the road because i am planning to have a writers' colony here at the farm with little cabins dotting the hillside where desperate but prolific folks can come and write that . . . book that will define our generation. . . . your friend, T___

I hope everyone gets to see this because I want you all to know how much I loved this class. What a wonderful, comfortable learning experience we shared. . . . What can I say? We inspire each other to greatness! . . . Maybe one day I'll visit the writer's colony and we'll schmooze over old days. . . . S___

One last note to say Good-bye. I feel sad. This has been a great class—my favorite this semester. I'm off to Washington D.C. in the morning—so I won't be on-line again with you. Good luck to everyone. . . . Love and peace, M___

The next semester, students from that class suggested an online graduate student conference, where all English graduate students could talk with each other and discuss their reading of works on the Graduate Reading List. It was a strong statement that a computer network could indeed enhance the study of literature in unexpected ways. The department has since begun implemented that suggestion, so that all graduate students in English will have MicroNet accounts during the course of their studies and access to an ongoing discussion of books required on the Graduate Reading List.

Research Online

Students in one online course concentrated their research on the effects of using computers for the teaching and study of literature. Some of the results of their work has been referred to in earlier chapters of this book, and several of their papers are collected in Appendix D. The papers demonstrate a little of what is available to the network-literate student, and what is possible when students are motivated to learn.

For example, two aspiring secondary teachers—Carla Beck and Shelley Sizemore—engaged in an online discussion of adolescent novels by Sue Ellen Bridgers. They then developed a dialogue with a class of middle school students who were involved in a BookRead Project led by long time BookRead Project teacher Nita Matzen. Finally, these pre-service teachers and the middle grade children entered into a real time, online chat with Sue Ellen Bridgers, all watching their screens from different locations in western North Carolina. These two teachers-to-be concluded that their experiment in collaborative learning had given them a distinct advantage as they anticipated having their own classrooms:

We have seen firsthand the excitement, involvement, and encouragement this type of communication brings into the English classroom. Using telecommunications to teach literature can link students to other students, authors, and as a result culminate in an "educational explosion."

We think that what they took part in could be called "electronic reader response."

Another research project, conducted by Scott Kemp (See Appendix D), used the network to survey other respondents on Internet literary discussion lists, in an effort to determine what impact the computer is having on the study of literature. As he points out:

> [The] medium itself provides the solution to the problem of gathering information about this potentially important supplemental tool to the study of English. . . . [O]nline interviews with the subscribers to the various literary lists . . . may collectively reveal the trends that are guiding the use of "Lit lists" among English colleagues, and demonstrate how the Lit list is changing the way we discuss . . . literature.

Another online research project on what is available to teachers of English through commercial online services was conducted by Randy Pitts, who also wrote on how to put technology into schools without breaking the budget (see Appendix D).

A former computer specialist turned poet, Pitts was also one of the judges for the WCU MicroNet poetry contest. The poems come to the contest via the network, from schools all over North Carolina. Students whose poems are chosen by their teachers for entry all receive a certificate; winners receive T-shirts and plaques with their poems prepared for mounting; students whose poems are selected for the final collection receive a copy of the book, as do their school libraries; and the three top winners' schools get plaques for display. The project, designed by WCU MicroNet's Bonnie Beam, gives graduate students like Randy Pitts a chance to mentor young writers, while it gives youngsters access to an outside expert, to an audience of their peers and fellow writers, and to a publishing opportunity: the writing process in action, electronically.

Research projects like these can give teachers and their students a way to collaborate in the learning process, a practice that is too often confined to the science laboratory or to thesis writing. With a network, students in any class requiring writing and research can have this extremely valuable kind of access to their teachers and their peers.

Tutorials, independent studies, and thesis supervision all work well by computer. The network is an easy means of scheduling face-to-face meetings as needed, as well as a way to communicate in the interim. The instructor becomes more acessible; so do the students. Telephone tag and meeting-time conflicts become dead issues.

One of the most dramatic examples of a successful tutorial course was a seminar for student teachers taught by Denise Heinze, one of our "critics-on-call." She introduced her English methods class to networking during one class period, allowing them to practice during the semester while they had immediate access to individual help from the WCU MicroNet staff on campus. In the following semester, when they were placed in schools as student teachers under her supervision, she and they kept in touch through WCU MicroNet. Placement at distant locations around rural western North Carolina had previously created difficulties for students and supervisors alike. Visits were limited by time, distance, weather, and mountainous terrain. Communication was hard to maintain. With networking, the students had easy access to their university supervisor as well as to each other. Professor Heinze could answer their questions on a daily basis, advise them individually, and post announcements for the group. The students could share the triumphs and disasters of their first classroom experiences and consult with each other on how they were solving common problems.

After the first year, students in the methods class corresponded with student teachers who were placed in the schools during the same semester, a rare opportunity to ask real questions about real situations that their peers were encountering while studying methods in class. Now, three years later, the student teachers' class conference is one of the liveliest and most useful on the network; others in the English department have begun to experiment with networking; and other departments are following suit in using the network for student teachers.

Individual Needs

For the individual student, networking can meet a variety of special needs. For example, one student took the short story course in the regular classroom, but added the dimension of networking in order to earn honors credit and at the same time correspond with students abroad, in preparation for her career goal—joining the Peace Corps. Another student, who had to drive a great distance over icy mountain roads, chose to take the course as an independent study through the network rather than at night on campus during the winter. One student, severely injured in an automobile accident and confined to a wheelchair with only limited use of his hands, was able to use a typing device to communicate by computer, becoming a fully active member of a class offered on the network.

Access for students whose schedule, location, job, physical condition, or home-bound responsibilities prevent class attendance at the usual location has been a real breakthrough. Education by telecommunication can meet students where they are. Future educational structures will include not only wide-area networking, but also the interactive use of all communication technologies—text, graphics, video, audio—and those yet to come.

Observations

Teaching courses on a computer network has been a continuing adventure for us, whether through independent studies for in-service teachers, regular literature courses on or off campus, or school-college projects such as the BookRead Project. As expected, most students have been eager to embrace the world of telecommunications, with less self-consciousness and less fear of failure than their elders. And also as expected, students have a much shorter learning curve! But after six years of teaching online, most of our early assumptions about the possibilities and pitfalls of this new mode of teaching have changed considerably.

The most obvious aspect of telecommunications—*speed*—still came as a surprise. Explanations had to be shorter and more to the point, information was accessible in more efficient ways than by the lecture method, and student-to-student interaction went on continuously, uninterrupted by a teacher-dominated environment. Frequently, students reread their assignments to find their own answers rather than asking the kinds of questions that take class time away from others. Or they answered each other's questions before the instructor could. The result was a more efficient use of time. And since much more could be accomplished in a week of telecommunicating than was possible in a few class meetings each week, the course content could be pursued in more depth or expanded to include more reading and writing.

A second realization was that we had much more real *access* to each other. The "classroom" and the "office door" remained open around the clock. Logging in every morning meant answering the day's e-mail, one-on-one, and responding to the class conference, where fierce discussions of the assignment had been under way while the instructor slept. It meant checking the database for recent entries on reading assignments and noting whether book discussion groups needed any interventions. Not only could every student have undivided attention and get a very quick response, but the instructor could leave a message for the errant few about missed assignments or deadlines. And best of all, the instructor could use private e-mail to confer with an individual student or make general comments to the whole class at once, long before small problems could become large ones.

We also learned that "information," as a name, was inadequate for describing the highway we were on. Certainly the network provided unparalled access to every kind of resource—libraries, texts, experts, and all. But for all of us, an equally real value was in *community*—all the communities that could exist, side by side, in limitless electronic space, as well as the sense of community that shared cyberspace could generate. Isolation created by location was dissolved. The students and the instructor could meet people of like interests all over the world.

Of course, being human, we would not choose to live by computer screen alone. We crave human contact. But communication across the barriers of space and time by telecommunications has in fact fostered personal contact, not replaced it. Isolated pen pals have met in person, groups of children have visited their peers in other schools and countries, experts in specialized fields have come together at meetings and conferences—all of them having found each other first in communities along that information highway.

7

Introduction to the World Wide Web

If we are to prepare our students for their tomorrows, we need to embrace the opportunities the Internet provides for new forms of literacy. No matter how technologically challenged any one of us feels, each of us must enter this new world and make every attempt to keep up with the changes taking place in what literacy means.

—Donald J. Leu, Jr.

Pardon My Metaphors

Is the "World Wide Web" the same thing as the "Internet"? Why a "Web" and a "Net"? How do you "surf" a net or a web or, for that matter, an "information superhighway"?

The mixed metaphors of computerese have become a regular part of standup comic routines ever since one television personality said he felt like "a roadkill on the information highway." Amusing as the wordplay is, many potential computer users are put off—and understandably so—by the confusing jargon and mysterious acronyms of "cyberspace." Let's just try for clarity with a few definitions and examples.

First, the Internet. As we said in Chapter 6, the Internet is simply a network of networks, the largest in the world. And a computer network is two or more computers connected to each other. Users can "get on" the Internet by connecting through a network that is already connected to the Internet—such as one at your school or office—or by dialing into an "Internet service provider"(just another network system), using their local or toll-free telephone number. These providers have proliferated enormously in the last few years and are advertised everywhere. From America Online to AT&T to your local yellow pages, you can certainly get there from where you are. And when a computer connects to the Internet, by whatever means, the "line" is open for communication with any of millions of other "sites" on the Internet around the world. (For more about the Internet, see Chapter 6.)

What then is the World Wide Web? The WWW (or "Web") is a large collection of "hypertext" documents on the Internet. And what are hypertext documents? They are documents that have been constructed with electronic "links"—pointers within the documents themselves—which lead to other documents. That is, they contain a set of electronic codes that make it possible to click a computer mouse on a picture or highlighted word in the text to call up another related document. For example, if you read a Web text on Jack London, a title like *The Call of the Wild* or an interesting aspect of London's life like "Wolf House" might be highlighted. You can click your mouse on either highlighted phrase and be taken to a completely different page about that subject. From that new page, you could jump back to where you were, or forward to other references that have been highlighted on the new page. It's a little like reading a footnote and having your wish come true—the reference is at your fingertips with just a click of the mouse. As you discover the magic of the Web, you'll find that it consists not only of texts, images, and graphics, but sound and video as well!

Web Tools

In order to use the Web, you need a "Web browser" like Netscape Navigator or Microsoft Explorer. These software programs make it possible to view Web sites so that the links that have been embedded actually appear as images, highlighted phrases, or words. Instead of plain text, what you will see are attractive "pages" with easy-to-understand pictures and highlighted phrases rather than text-only menus, lists, and commands. As you click on these links, they will change color as they lead you into the world of the

Web, leaving a personalized trail through the maze of interconnected documents as you move around within them.

Your journey through this wealth of materials is made simpler and more focused by "search engines" (automated research assistants) that scan the contents of the Web by subject or other specified search word and create searchable catalogs. Yahoo, Altavista, HotBot, WebCrawler, Lycos, and InfoSeek are just a few of the search engines that will be available on your browser. Using any one of them, you might type an author's name—"Jack London"—in the Search Box, then click on the "search" button. The search engine will return a list of all of the "Jack London" references indexed on that search engine's system—in a matter of seconds. You may receive notice that the search has turned up many thousands of "hits"—sites that match what you are looking for. As in any research, narrowing your focus will lead more efficiently to the specific kinds of information you want. For help in using just the right search words, you will find among the tools on your browser at least a basic list of ways to focus your search more closely. Once you discover a promising site and type the Web address in the location box, you will be "on the Web." At that point the most useful tool on your browser is one that allows you to keep track of your journey by filing addresses of useful sites. Netscape calls this file "Bookmarks" while Explorer names it "Favorites."

Of course, no one index, list, or search engine covers the entire Internet, any more than the *Reader's Guide to Periodical Literature* indexes all of the world's periodicals. But among the many lists, indexes, and search engines now online, a useable map of the Internet world is beginning to emerge. If you were looking for Jack London somewhere on that map of the Web, your search might take you to far more distant places than Jack himself ever traveled. Along the way, you would encounter navigational decisions, learn travel tricks, and discover "sites" to see. The following sample search illustrates what might happen on such a journey.

Looking for Jack London: A Sample Search

The best way to begin this adventure is to arm yourself with some basic instruction on effective search techniques. Whole books have been written on the subject and deserve your attention. For example, *The Research*

Paper and the World Wide Web by Dawn Rodrigues is a good one to have on your reference shelf (For more, see our Bibliography). And there are brief online guides as well, such as "How to Search the World Wide Web: A Tutorial and Guide for Beginners," by Robert L. Balliot and David P. Habib (**http://www.ultranet.com/~egrlib/tutor.htm**). Another guide online is "Windweaver's Search Guide," by Tracy Marks (**http://www.windweaver.com/searchguide.htm**). Do read one. Any of them will save you days of aimless wandering.

What we are looking for is material for a research project on Jack London and the Gold Rush. Having read "To Build a Fire," what we want to find is something about the setting relative to London's personal experience of it. With guides in hand, we'll start by doing a subject search, then a keyword search using Yahoo (**http://www.yahoo.com**). The words in the subject will be in quotation marks, "Jack London," so that we don't get a zillion irrelevant references to both "Jack" and "London." Computers don't know the difference. Since Yahoo is one of the search tools that has allied subject and keyword search capability, we'll follow the subject search with a keyword search, locating more specific references to London's work about the Far North.

In order to tell the computer how keywords are relevant to the search, some other commands may be needed, like ANDs and ORs, NOTs and NEARs. They specify what terms must or must not be in the document for the selection to be made. (There are other command forms that can be used, like plus and minus signs. See your guides and the Help sections of specific search tools to choose what works best.) Without such guideposts, your screen will be filled with irrelevant references. A combination of the author's name in quotation marks and the word Klondike with the word "AND" placed immediately before it—ANDKlondike, with no space between—will work for our first keyword search.

Using the subject search word "Jack London, " Yahoo shows us twenty-eight appropriate sites (Figure 1). Other search tools will yield varying numbers of results, from hundreds to thousands.

By clicking on any appropriate highlighted phrase, we can go to the places listed and see what turns up next. In this case, we can choose "Jack London Collection" (Figure 2).

Wow! On this page we already have a brief biographical sketch and a list of places to go for more. The words | Contents | What's New | Biography || Audio & Video | Documents |Images | Writings | Research Aids |

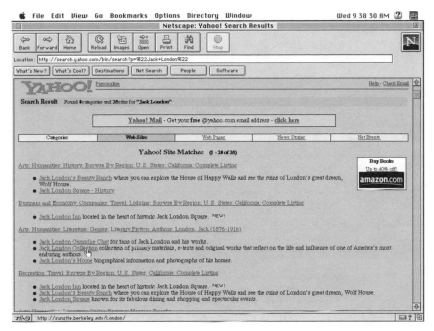

Figure 1   Subject search.

Figure 2   Subject search, stage two.

Figure 3   Keyword search.

Organizations | Listserv | Links | Search are all highlighted. Scroll down the page and there's an explanation of the categories represented by the highlighted words, followed by an invitation at the end of the page to "search the entire Jack London Collection by keyword(s)." We can come back to that—an easy task, since there's a function on the browser that lets us go back to where we were. But let's search this site for "Klondike" and see where that leads (Figure 3).

This search gave us nine hits, including a link to Jack London's Writings (Figure 4).

Another click and we have the Lost Face collection with the story "To Build a Fire" (Figure 5).

A click on that link will lead us right to the short story itself, with its intriguing description of exactly where the man on the trail was located:

> The man flung a look back along the way he had come. . . . North and south, as far as his eye could see, it was unbroken white, save for a dark hair-line that curved and twisted from around the spruce-covered island to the south, and

Figure 4 Keyword search, stage two.

Figure 5 Keyword search, stage three.

that curved and twisted away into the north, where it disappeared behind another spruce-covered island. This dark hair-line was the trail—the main trail—that led south five hundred miles to the Chilcoot Pass, Dyea, and salt water; and that led north seventy miles to Dawson, and still on to the north a thousand miles to Nulato, and finally to St. Michael on Bering Sea, a thousand miles and half a thousand more.

At this point, rather than reading further, we'll use the Edit function to select and copy the story to the Clipboard, then paste it from there to a word-processing window where it will be available to read at leisure, offline, or to print out. And before leaving the network, we'll make sure we've Bookmarked the sites we want to return to.

Having begun the search, we already know how much more is available online, not only in online documents, but also in the libraries we can access where books and articles can be found and retrieved. We can join the list mentioned on the site for an online discussion about Jack London with other teachers and students. One good question there might lead to dozens of suggestions. As you conduct your search, remember, of course, when it comes to computers, it's always "easier done than said!"

Classroom Connections

For those of us involved with children and their books, a wealth of information and opportunity for classroom research and enrichment are available on the Web. We describe some of the most useful Web addresses accessible at this writing to get you started. However, Web sites are added and deleted almost daily, and once you get hooked on the search, you are sure to find favorites of your own. As you investigate the sites listed below, you will notice many repetitions. That is because authors of Web pages are eager to connect their cyberspace readers with additional information, and they provide links to interesting sites they themselves have discovered. Hence, many Web pages link to one another. This is actually a good thing, since the sites that appear most frequently in this chain of links are probably the best of the lot—ones we can return to again and again as valuable resources for our teaching.

As Beth Baldwin states, technology can "totally transform our teaching," (Williams 41), for it gives us the opportunity to foster independence in our students, to shift the focus from a teacher-to-student paradigm to one in which the students take responsibility for their learning by engaging in their own research in areas that interest them and sharing that research with class members and even with peers beyond the classroom walls. Teaching with the Web means we have to master at least the basics of its operation, while at the same time being comfortable with the fact that many of our students will outdistance us in computer knowledge and expertise. Once we have established this level of comfort and trust, there are countless ways in which our students can use the Web. Whether they are engaged in an author study online or in the classroom, they can contact the author's publisher on the Web for information about the author. The author may even have a home page students can consult for a biography, bibliography, the answers to most frequently asked questions, a discussion of the author's writing process, and so forth. Once they have an author's biography in hand, students might wish to investigate certain aspects of the author's life, that is, look up information on the Web about the state or city in which the author was born, the author's college, and so forth. There are sites that provide booktalks about the author's books as well as published reviews of their merits. Students can look through the many special awards books lists such as the Caldecott and Newbery on the Web to determine whether any of their author's books have been so honored. Students can even write their own reviews of these books and add them to Web sites. They might compare various Web sources of information about an author for accuracy, thus helping them to become discerning researchers. In addition to engaging in research on the Web, students can synthesize what they have learned and construct their own Web pages. This will enable them to share their knowledge with a wider audience, and receive feedback and additional information from readers. They may even wish to try writing in the author's style and post some of their pieces on their Web page. Students can also participate in discussion forums.

Teachers can find most of what they need on the Web to prepare classes without leaving their desks. Local and college libraries, and even the Library of Congress, have sites that can put us in touch with annotated lists of books on a particular subject. One can even find entire texts of both classic and contemporary literature online, enabling teachers with large-screen projection capabilities to highlight passages for class discussion, search for themes, and so forth. Folklore, poetry, fiction, and nonfiction—all the literary genres we teach are amply represented on the Web. There are research services such as ERIC that will provide information on children's books or other aspects of the language arts. Many sites offer lesson plans, bibliographies of books organized by theme, in-depth discussions of issues related to teaching or issues in children's literature, even syllabi of others who teach the same subject. With all the Internet discussion groups now in operation, there is certain to be one tailored to the specific interests of any interested teachers. These discussion groups are places to share ideas, ask for help, and to learn more about a particular subject. Fortified with connections to this vast network of people and ideas, teachers can offer their students a wide variety of information on any topic they explore together through the school year. "Certainly, technology offers delicious possibilities for the classroom" (Williams, 41).

A Selected List of Web Sites Related to the Language Arts

50 Great Web Sites for Kids and Parents
http://www.ssdesign.com/parentspage/greatsites/50.html

This address includes a wealth of sites for students, teachers, and parents, with links to still more sites. Many different subjects are represented, and there are several that relate to the language arts. Among the many treats is a rather sophisticated page created by a twelve-year-old about Brian Jacques, author of the wildly popular Redwall fantasy series. This page might serve as an excellent model for students who wish to create their own Web pages. It also has a link to a lesson plan by Carol Otis Hurst for using Redwall books in the classroom. In addition, there are sites that provide lists of excellent books for all ages, and booktalks written by children.

Achuka Children's Books UK
http://www.home.fastnet.co.uk/mthorn

Since many British authors are published by American publishers, teachers might be interested in this site, which treats children's books and children's book publishing in the U.K. There are no links to other sites. Rather, this page gives a complete picture of publishing trends, the latest books in a variety of genres, award winners, and more.

ALAN Review
http://scholar.lib.vt.edu/ejournals/ALAN/winter97/w97-toc.html

This site provides a recent edition of *ALAN Review,* a journal for teachers and librarians working with adolescents. There are articles related to literature for young adults, many by or about authors who write for this age group, as well as reviews of young adult literature.

Association of Library Services to Children
http://www.ala.org/alsc/

The Association provides lists of their award-winning books such as the Caldecott, Newbery, and Notables, and information on useful sites for children and teachers.

Banyan Tree Friends
http://sashimi.wwa.com/~uschwarz/poetry/btf000.html

This site contains an extensive collection of student poetry. Readers can search a database for poems by state, school, grade level, or the name of the poet.

Booktalks Quick and Simple
http://www.concord.k12.nh.us/schools/rundlett/booktalks

In this interesting site for teachers and librarians, over four hundred booktalks are arranged alphabetically by author and by book. Most are a few sentences long, but some books receive a more lengthy treatment. Age and interest level for the books are also included. While these talks are merely summaries and do not contain the drama and suspense that might be necessary to entice potential readers, they do provide busy teachers and librarians with a good base from which to craft their own talks for children. The Web author welcomes additions to the database and gives credit to those who submit booktalks.

The Bulletin of the Center for Children's Books
http://edfu.lis.uiuc.edu/puboff/bccb/

This is an online version of the excellent children's book review publication, complete with a listing of their recommended books, in-depth discussions of featured books, and so forth.

Carol Hurst's Children's Literature Site
http://www.carolhurst.com/

Authored by children's literature consultants and professional writers Rebecca Otis and Carol Hurst, this site is rich in information. For several featured books, the authors provide a teaching guide that includes a review; things to notice and talk about; activities; related books; and related areas in the site. An expanded list of recommended books and reviews is also helpful. The authors provide a list of professional books and articles as well.

The Children's Book Council
http://www.cbcbooks.org/

The Council provides information on its services as well as many book lists, including science and nature titles, books with marvelous images, books about art and artists, and so forth.

Children's Literature Authors and Illustrators
http://www.ucet.ufl.edu/~jbrown/chauth.html

This site contains information on over one hundred children's authors and illustrators. In addition, there are links to related pages such as children's books online, publishers, authors' and illustrators' birthdays, and so forth.

The Children's Literature Home Page
http://www.parentsplace.com/readroom/childnew/index.html

This site helps teachers find the best children's books available by offering hundreds of online reviews of both print and multi media materials, special bibliographies, lists of award-winning books, and more.

Children's Literature Sources on the Internet
http://www.edu.yorku.ca/~tcs/~adawson/childlit.html

Here in one place are links to many of the wonderful sites described in this chapter as well as a link to multicultural book reviews and a storytelling link that provides the full text for many stories of different varieties, such as stories for the holidays, myths and legends, and so forth.

The Children's Literature Web Guide
http://www.ucalgary.ca/~dkbrown/index.html

Once you investigate this site, you'll wonder how you ever lived without it! Compiled by David K. Brown, Director of the Doucette Library of Teaching Resources at the University of Calgary, the Web Guide is just that—a guide to just about everything involving children's literature on the Web. Especially helpful is the "Resources for Teachers" link that provides access to lesson plans, storytelling, and more. In addition, there are lists of award-winning books, gopher sites (guides to Internet directories organized by subject), publishers, authors, discussion groups, teaching guides and ideas, children's literature journals and other publications, children's literature organizations, and so much more. A good number of other children's literature sites appear as links here.

Education World
http://www.education-world.com/

Educators can search a database of more than fifty thousand reviewed Web sites. In addition, there are links to themed lesson plans, monthly book reviews, articles on professional development—even topics of interest to administrators.

The Educator's Toolkit
http://www.eagle.ca/~matink/

There are many applications for the language arts teacher in this site. There is a link to the "Resources for Teachers" at the Children's Literature Web Guide site, as well as an interesting project called "Writers in Electronic Residence"—writers who help classes of children in Canada with their writing.

Electronic Resources for Youth Services
http://chebucto.ns.ca/Education/ERYS/online.html#top

An interesting site that includes texts of fairy tales and stories, bibliographies of children's books, and, especially useful, a link to a site that publishes children's writing online.

Fairrosa Cyber Library of Children's Literature
http://www.users.interport.net/~fairrosa/index.html

This very useful site contains bibliographies of books by theme, information on authors and illustrators, book reviews, and links to other children's literature sites. What makes it unique is a compilation of the major discussion themes from the wonderful childlit e-mail discussion group of teachers, librarians, and others interested in children's literature.

Inkspot
http://www.inkspot.com/author/

Meant as a source of information for beginning writers, this site is rich in other information as well. There is a link to author interviews on Amazon.com; advice for beginning writers from many published authors, including writers for children; a directory of authors who visit schools; and much more.

Internet Public Library Youth Division
http://www.ipl.org/youth/WorldReading/

Designed to be like walking into a local library, this site provides students with information on a variety of subjects and the opportunity to participate in discussing many of them. In addition to information about books and authors, there is an interesting Read to Write Project in which participants read an online literary selection; join a discussion about the qualities of writing in the genre selected; apply those qualities to their own writing; and get published on the Web. Participants can see a list of others in the project, find out something about them, and even locate on a map the areas in which participants live.

K-12 Internet Test Bed
http://www.cpb.org/edtech/k12testbed/proposal.ktsc.html

This site describes proposals for ten Internet-based educational networking projects around the nation. Reading some of these proposals can give you an idea of the incredible possibilities for actively involving students in the learning process and providing a wide audience for their reading and writing.

Kathy Schrock's Guide for Educators—
Literature and Language Arts
http://www.capecod.net/schrockguide/arts/artlit.htm

This is an incredible site filled with links to many other worthwhile language arts sites described in this chapter. In addition, it contains a link to all the works of Shakespeare online, complete with a glossary of terms; essays and information on early seventeenth century literature; a Dante Gabriel Rossetti archive; an archive of poetry written before 1920; teachers' guides to over sixty novels published by Bantam, Doubleday, and Dell; and links to searches for hundreds of books online.

Kay Vandergrift's Special Interest Page
http://www.scils.rutgers.edu/special/kay/kayhp2.html

Kay Vandergrift is a professor at Rutgers University, New Jersey, whose site is an incredible resource with numerous links. She has a children's literature site as well as many special topic sites, including a page on linking literature with learning across the curriculum; an in-depth study of *Snow White;* a study of the 1997 Caldecott winner, *Golem;* abundant information on authors, book selection materials; and more.

KidPub
http://www.kidpub.org/kidpub/>

Students may submit stories to this site as well as participate in a chat room, complete with role-playing capabilities.

KidzPage
http://web.aimnet.com/~veeceet/kids/kidzpage.html

This poetry site contains a variety of poems, ranging from works by famous poets to original works by students and teachers.

LibraryLand
http://www.rcls.org/libland

While this site is primarily for librarians, language arts teachers can find much of interest to them. There are many links to other worthwhile sites, including David K. Brown's Children's Literature Web Guide, and uncommon bibliographies such as "Gay and Lesbian Characters and Themes in Children's Books" and "Children's Books about Jewish Religion and Culture." Teachers who encourage storytelling in their classes will appreciate the storytelling links in this site.

Native American Technology and Art (Poems and Stories)
http://www.nativeweb.org/NativeTech/poetry/

Poems shaped by Native American experiences make up this site. Accompanied by illustrations, the selections are divided into sections called "Beavers and Beyond" and "Medicine Dreams."

National Council of Teachers of English (NCTE)
http://www.ncte.org/idea/list.html

In addition to information about NCTE, this site offers teaching ideas and resources, parent and community resources, English Language Arts Standards, and much more.

The Online Books Page
http://www.cs.cmu.edu/booklists.html

This page offers the possibility of searching by title and author over four thousand complete texts online.

The New York Times on the Web: Books
http://www.nytimes.com/books/home/

Readers can search reviews from the *New York Times Book Review* back to 1980. This is an incredible resource!

Positively Poetry
http://iquest.com/~e-media/kv/poetry.html

Developed by a thirteen-year-old girl, this site provides a place where students can read poetry by their peers around the world and also publish their own poems.

The Shiki Internet Haiku Salon
http://cc.matsuyama-u.ac.jp/~shiki/

At this award-winning site, the art of haiku is explained in detail, using original Japanese haiku and translations as examples. There are lesson plans and beautiful accompanying artwork. Poets may also post their own poems.

Vocabulary University
http://www.Vocabulary.com

Students may enjoy increasing their vocabulary painlessly by participating in the monthly vocabulary word puzzles available on this site.

A Few Author Sites

Caroline Arnold
http://www.geocities.com/Athens/1264

Avi
http://www.avi-writer.com/

Byrd Baylor
http://www.simonsays.com/kidzone/auth/bbaylor.html

Shonto Begay
hozhogo95@aol.com

Joan Blos
http://www.simonsays.com/kidzone/auth/jblos.html

Jan Brett
http://www.janbrett.com/

Ashley Bryan
http://www.simonsays.com/kidzone/auth/abryan.html

Eve Bunting
http://www.econoclad.com/newsletters/bunting.html

Eric Carle
http://www.eric-carle.com/

Vicki Cobb
http://www.web-shop.com/vcobb/tablecon.html

Barbara Cooney
http://www.penguin.com/usa/childrens/bios/cooney.html

Tomie dePaola
http://www.opendoor.com/bingley/mywebpage.html

Leo and Diane Dillon
http://www.inkspot.com/illus/dillon.html

Jerry Emery
jerryemery@aol.com

Mary Downing Hahn
http://www.carr.lib.md.us/authco/hahn.htm

Virginia Hamilton
http://members.aol.com/bodeep/index.html

Kevin Henkes
http://www.penguin.com/usa/childrens/bios/henkes.htm

Patrick Jennings
lgill1l@bisbeepl.lib.az.us

Jackie French Koller
http://members.aol.com/jackiek/index.htm

Kathryn Lasky
kathlask1@aol.com

Julius Lester
http://www.penguin.com/usa/childrens/bios/lester.htm

Lois Lowry
http://ipl.sils.umich.edu/youth/AskAuthor/Lowry.html

Mary Lyons
http://www.comet.net/writersc/lyonsden/

Suse MacDonald
suse@sovernet
http://www.create4kids.com

James Marshall
http://www.penguin.com/usa/childrens/bios/marshall.htm

Norma Fox Mazer
readNFM@aol.com

Michael McCurdy
mmccurdy@ben.net
http://www.ben.net/~mmccurdy/

Katherine Paterson
http://www.terabithia.com/

Gary Paulsen
http://www.bdd.com/forum/bddforum.cgi/trc/index/paul

Richard Peck
http://www.penguin.com/usa/childrens/bios/peck.htm

Jerry Pinkney
http://www.penguin.com/usa/childrens/bios/pinkney.htm

Patricia Polacco
**http://www.mca.com/putnam/authors/patricia_polacco/author
.html**

Adam Rapp
rapp@frontstreetbooks.com

Jon Scieszka
http://www.penguin.com/usa/childrens/bios/jon.htm

Maurice Sendak
http://homearts.com/depts/relat/sendakf1.htm

Janet Stevens
http://www.ucalgary.ca/~dkbrown/jstevens.html

Chris Van Allsburg
http://www.penguin.com/usa/childrens/bios/chris.htm

E. B. White
http://www.tiac.net/users/winlib/ebwhite.htm

David Wisniewski
http://www.carr.lib.md.us/authco/wisn.htm

Jane Yolen
yolen@aol.com

Ed Young
**http://www.putnam.com/putnam/authors/ed_young/
author.html**

Publishers' Web Sites

In addition to many other features, these sites are a rich source of information about authors and illustrators.

Chelsea House
http://www.ChelseaHouse.com

DK Publishing
http://www.dk.com/

Front Street Books
http://www.frontstreetbooks.com/

Gareth Stevens Publishing
http://Literary.COM//gsinc/index.html

HarperCollins Children's Books
http://www.harperchildrens.com/index.htm

Houghton Mifflin's children's book page
http://www.hmco.com/hmco/trade/childrens/index.html

Houghton Mifflin's Reading Language Arts Center
http://www.eduplace.com/rdg/index.html
One of the interesting features of this page is the ability of teachers to participate in several discussion forums.

Little Brown Books for Children
http://www.pathfinder.com/@@2f6@mQcARAJpILXm/twep/lb _childrens/index.html

Multicultural Publishing and Education Council
http://www.quiknet.com/mbt/mpec/mpec.html

Penguin USA Children's Books
http://www.penguin.com/usa/childrens/index.html

Puffin Books
http://www.puffin.co.uk/Puffin/thepuffinhouse.html

Random House Books for Young Readers
http://www.randomhouse.com/cats/youngreaders.html

Reading Online
http://www.readingonline.org

Available via paid subscription, this is an online professional periodical published by the International Reading Association (IRA). It consists of seven sections: Critical Issues, Developments in Literacy, The Electronic Classroom, Graduate Students, International Forum, Professional Materials, and Research.

Scholastic
http://www.scholastic.com

Where Do We Go from Here?

We are at the beginning of a new age in education. As the next millennium arrives, we will see our world transformed in many ways by electronic communication. The speed of Internet connections is almost beyond imagination already as ISDN (Integrated Services Digital Network), a high-speed digital telephone connection, develops. And not far in the future, cable modems and satellite connections will boggle the mind. With the advent of wireless networks, which are already available experimentally in infrared and radio frequency, it will be possible to connect to a network from a portable computer with the ease of pointing a remote control at a television set. In fact, WebTV already exists, available from Philips Magnavox. Voice-driven computing is at hand, as are such exotics as virtual reality headsets. The results in multiplied access points are obvious.

Electronic mail, the most widely used of the Internet's services, already connects students around the world, who are communicating with each other about immediate issues and developments, from wars in remote countries to pollution around the globe. And classrooms of the very near future will see widespread use of the kinds of projects that are currently under way only as experiments in schools around the country:

Distance learning, with an instructor teaching students at multiple sites via two-way video and audio;

Online research accessing the best of libraries and news sources everywhere;

Home/school communication that allows home tutoring, homework hotlines, and parent involvement;

Video teleconferences linking students in town meetings by video, telephone and fax;

Collaborative learning projects where students from different cultures create joint projects or learn foreign languages from each other by two-way video;

Video field trips via live television to places as remote as outer space and under the sea;

Interactive television shows, like quiz programs, that can involve viewers in the action

We can expect telecommunications to be the premier preservice and inservice learning center of the future for teachers. Teachers will take courses, observe master classrooms, consult with other educators, and conference with other schools in this new world of learning opportunities, using all of the electronic media we know of now, as well as technology that is now in the planning stages.

Ernest L. Boyer, President of the Carnegie Foundation for the Advancement of Teaching, names technology as one of the five priorities to consider in reforming education. In "Shaping the Future: A Five Point Plan for Education Reform," he writes:

> If we could blend electronic images with great teachers and books, and use computers as learning tools, America could, in the next century, have the most outstanding education system in the world. (66)

We agree. Every part of the equation Boyer describes is essential for the future of education—computers, books, and, most of all, great teachers.

Author Chats on BookRead

Excerpt from a Chat with Sue Ellen Bridgers

The following dialogue is a sample of an online chat among students and teachers at Smokey Mountain High School, Sylva, North Carolina (Mustangs); Tuscola High School, Waynesville, North Carolina; North Buncombe High School, Weaverville, North Carolina; and author Sue Ellen Bridgers.

;; MUSTANGS (tty3A): Hi sueellen.

;;; sueellen (tty3i): Hey! SEB

;; nbuncomb (tty3C): Hi, Sueellen, What inspired you to write books about kids with problems?

;;; sueellen (tty3i): Hi. Kids without problems don't make for good or even interesting books.

;;; MUSTANGS (tty3A): How were you able to make the drug scene so authentic in pc [*Permanent Connections*]?

;; sueellen (tty3i): So you want to know if I did drugs, huh? Well, you'll never know. Writers don't have to have had all the experiences they write about. I talked to people, read about it, of course, and have seen drug use on film.

;;; nbuncomb (tty3C): Why did you end Notes . . . with Wren's dad still in the hospital?

;;; sueellen (tty3i): Because that seemed to be the most realistic conclusion to me. Wren and Kevin dealing with it was the real issue, not Tom's recovery. In other words, the book was about them, not him.

;;; MUSTANGS (tty3A): What is purpose of Coralee? Couldn't the story have been the same without her?

;;; sueellen (tty3i): Nothing can be the same with a part missing. Coralee was there because when I envisioned the house, she was in it. She and Ginny also provided a view of women in relationship, just as Leanna and Ellery show relationship between younger women.

;;; nbuncomb (tty3C): What was the cause of Tom's illness in Notes . . . ?

;;; sueellen (tty3i): I don't really know. My father suffered from a similar illness and there's still little understanding of what causes a normal healthy person to suddenly become depressed. Probably some kind of chemical imbalance.

;;; MUSTANGS (tty3A): Rob asked his father for a phone card as part of the deal to stay. Why does he never use it? Is he just seeing how far he can push his father or did you forget to have him use it?

;;; sueellen (tty3i): I don't even remember that he asked for it—I assume you guys know. Maybe. Actually, if characters in a book do in the course of a day what real people do, the book would be very long and boring. So the writer picks and chooses what to record, trying to get those moments that are significant and avoiding ones that aren't. I guess I didn't think using the card meant anything to the story.

;;; nbuncomb (tty3C): In PC, was Rob entirely fictional?

;;; sueellen (tty3i): Rob was an invention in the sense that I don't know him personally, but he's like a lot of guys. When I first envisioned him in my mind, he was stoned and I figured if I was going to get to know him at all I'd better get him out of Montclair and into an environment where he had to do something about himself.

;;; MUSTANGS (tty3A): There are people in our class who want to write short stories but have no idea how to begin. Any suggestions?

;;; sueellen (tty3i): I can only describe my own process. I envision a character in a situation and from that get a sense of what the story is. Then I wait awhile, thinking about it, letting my subconscious do a lot of the work, so when I start writing, the story seems to be at least partially written in my head. Often, young (new) writers try to write too soon—a great idea that doesn't have time to "stew" ends out being just a great idea and not a story.

;;; tuscola (tty3D): In the book Home Before Dark, did Stella in the book represent your life as a teenager?

;;; sueellen (tty3i): No. I was not a migrant child. I grew up in a small town in eastern N.C. and we had migrant children in our school from time to time. I was always interested in them but never got to know any of them very well. Stella was an attempt to get into the head of a kid like that.

;;; nbuncomb (tty3C): How old are your own children and how do they relate to your books?

;;; sueellen (tty3i): My children are 28, 26, 24 years old. When they were younger, I made a real point of not using them or anything that happened to them in the books. Now they're all too old to be of any interest.

;;; MUSTANGS (tty3A): In the book pc you spent chapter 17 having Ginny remember playing with dolls when she was 8. Why. . . .

;;; sueellen (tty3i): Because I wanted to deal with the issue of motherhood just a little bit. The problems between mother and daughter were important to the story.

;;; tuscola (tty3D): I would like to know if any of the migrant children that you did know prompted you to write your book Home Before Dark.

;;; sueellen (tty3i): Actually, it was one I didn't know that prompted the character of Stella. I regretted not getting to know a girl who I think was probably feisty and stubborn the way Stella was.

;;; nbuncomb (tty3C): Any plans for movies from your books?

;;; sueellen (tty3i): There are always plans for movies. Right now, the active one is for All Together Now. If I got excited about all the movie deals I hear about, I'd be a nervous wreck. Movie people are CRAZY!

;;; MUSTANGS (tty3B): Do so many of your characters have mental illnesses to help you deal with your father's mental illness?

;;; sueellen (tty3i): I think Tom is the only character I've written about with a mental illness. I thought writing the book would help me but I don't think it did—after all I was grown when I wrote it and the issues of being a teenager with a mentally ill parent were pretty much resolved by then.

;;; tuscola (tty3D): If you were to write a new book, would you do it on your real life and the times you had?

;;; **sueellen (tty3i):** I'm always writing a new book and so far none of them have been about my own life. I haven't had a very interesting life, I don't guess, at least it doesn't seem especially book-worthy to me.

;;; **tuscola (tty3D):** Well, not knowing about your life might make some people wonder how and where you grew up.

;;; **sueellen (tty3i):** I grew up in eastern N.C. All that kind of information is available in research books, like Ted Hipple's PRESENTING SUE ELLEN BRIDGERS and lots of issues of the ALAN REVIEW which should be available in your school library.

Excerpt from a Chat with Jean Craighead George

The following dialogue is a sample of a computer conversation among students at Leadmine Elementary School, Raleigh, North Carolina; Port Chester Middle School, Port Chester, New York; Whitby School, Greenwich, Connecticut; and author Jean Craighead George. Although the teacher's user name (saccardi) identifies Whitby School, student representatives actually typed their peers' questions and comments. "Johnson" is the MicroNet systems operator at Western Carolina University.

;;;**jeancg (tty3B):** Hello, I'm here.

;;;**johnson (tty02):** I shall now rescind my "throne" & hand it over to you guys. . . .

;;; **leadmine (tty3C):** Is there no hope for the old Eskimo ways found in Julie of the Wolves? I ask this because you say Julie pointed her boots toward Kapugen.

;;; **jeancg (tty3B):** Yes, there is hope. Some of the educated and well-respected Eskimos are teaching Inupiat, basket making from baleen and dancing. The old ceremonies are being observed.

;;; **saccardi (tty3D):** Jean, where did you get the idea for the moon books, especially the gray wolves?

;;; **jeancg (tty3B):** My editor asked me to write a series. Lying in bed one night I heard an owl call in January; and thought about the 13 lunar months. I sat up in bed. An animal for each lunar month I said to myself, and thought of each one and what certain animals were doing at the time. The wolf pups are on their own in November. The owl was building a nest and courting his mate in January.

;;; leadmine (tty3C): Do you name the animals in your stories after people you know?

;;; jeancg (tty3B): No, not the animals. But many of the people are friends of mine.

;;; ptcheste (tty3A): Aren't the salamanders wild and dangerous?

;;; jeancg (tty3B): Yes, salamanders are all around us in the east, but they are endangered because we are building in their woodland habitats. I have had many experiences. Every year I go out on the first spring rain after the spring thaw. I go to the woods in boots and raincoat and watch the primordial march of these glorious creatures. It's thrilling because they've been doing this for at least 300 million years.

;;; leadmine (tty3C): Why did Kapugen kill the wolves when they once helped him?

;;; jeancg (tty3B): Kapugen killed the wolves because Eskimos are very practical. They must survive. The seals and whales were gone. A white man offered money to go shoot wolves. But you know what? You've just given me a terrific idea for the sequel! Wow!

;;; ptcheste (tty3A): Is Myax representative of the archetype of man who is one with the nature of the Earth?

;;; jeancg (tty3B): Myax does represent man and nature taking care of one another.

;;; saccardi (tty3D): You seem to know a lot about sharks. Have you had any experiences with them?

;;; jeancg (tty3B): I'll talk about sharks. Yes, I spent several months on an island in the Sea of Cortez, Mexico, with my son, Luke, and the shark fishermen, Ramon, Ramon II, and Tomas. A shark scared me to death!

;;; leadmine (tty3C): When they made the movie My Side of the Mountain, did you have any say in it? We were disappointed.

;;; jeancg (tty3B): Leadmine, I didn't have anything to do with the movie of My Side. Hollywood wishes authors would fade away.

;;; ptcheste (tty3A): Is Shark Beneath the Reef the most popular book of yours? If not, which one is?

;;; jeancg (tty3B): No, My Side of the Mountain is; also Julie of the Wolves.

;;; saccardi (tty3D): Are there any more well-established Seminole Indian tribes?

;;; jeancg (tty3B): Yes, like other American Indians, the Seminoles are trying to find their place in a modern culture and teach their children the old ways as well. Buffalo Tiger is a Seminole leader who is keeping his heritage alive—but it is difficult.

;;; saccardi (tty3D): Why did you have Mandy kill Nina Terrance, why didn't you have Nina fly away?

;;; jeancg (tty3B): I had a crow—and they can be vindictive—who attacked a little girl who had kicked him. I did not shoot the crow, but I took it far away. People do come first, even though I love animals.

;;; leadmine (tty3C): Have you ever seen a mountain lion in front of a doorstep as in One Day in the Desert?

;;; jeancg (tty3B): No, but my niece raised a mountain lion cub, and returned it to the den many months later.

;;; saccardi (tty3D): Do you like to write only adventure books? Do you prefer to write fact or fiction books?

;;; jeancg (tty3B): I am a nature writer; that is a new genre of literature. It is fact or fiction with a poetic interpretation of nature and a scientific point of view.

Excerpt from a Chat with Gary Paulsen

A computer conversation among students and teachers from Port Chester Middle School, Port Chester, NY; Whitby School, Greenwich, CT; and author Gary Paulsen, in northern Minnesota. Although the teacher's user name (saccardi) identifies Whitby School, student representatives actually typed their peers' questions and comments. "Johnson" is the MicroNet systems operator at Western Carolina University.

paulsen: Hello—is anybody out there?

saccardi: Hi, we're here and reading you loud and clear.

johnson: Gary—Hope you like this medium. . . . We're all still getting used to it ourselves.

paulsen: Agreed. I'm worried that I'm going to blurt out something wrong here. It's kind of fun, though, isn't it?

saccardi: Gary, how often do you write?

paulsen: I work all the time. I get up at four thirty in the morning, meditate for half an hour, then start working. Not always writing but working. If I'm not writing I read and study and continue to study until I fall asleep at night. Now, with all this film stuff going on, I have to watch movies sometimes but not so often. Mostly I just read and write.

saccardi: In the book, The Night the White Deer Died, how did you write so well from the point of view of a girl? Did you have help?

paulsen: Not in that way. I had a friend who had a young daughter and he helped me a bit but mostly I just observed, tried to think as I thought a girl would think, and studied people. I have since written a book called the MADONNA STORIES which is an attempt to understand the feminine aspect to life. It is a book of short stories.

saccardi: What style of writing do you have, what kind of books do you read, who are your favorite authors?

paulsen: I don't know what kind of style I have. I think it changes all the time as I learn and (I hope) grow. I am now discovering more about writing, how the rhythms and pulses work, and that changes things a lot as I work. I don't have favorite authors so much as favorite books. Moby Dick, The Color Purple, some of Steinbeck but not all, some of Hemingway but not all—books here and there. My favorite books are good ones and they are few and far between.

saccardi: On the average, Gary, how long does it take you to write a book and which one took the longest?

paulsen: It isn't a question of time. For instance, the writing of Dogsong took maybe three or four months. But I have twenty-two thousand miles on sleds in the Arctic and Canada and Alaska to learn enough for the book. All together I maybe have six, seven years of work in that one book that I wrote in three or four months. The typing of a book is nothing, compared to the living of it. The longest book I have ever written was for Prentice-Hall and it was called THE BUYING A NEW, REMODELING A USED, BUILDING YOUR OWN COMPREHENSIVE HOME SHELTER AND HOW TO DO IT BOOK. It was so boring . . . well, never mind. Six hundred and twelve pages.

ptchestr: Why did you decide to write books instead of making movies?

paulsen: They are two different things, movies and books, and I do both. Hatchet is a film which I wrote—they changed the title to A CALL IN THE WILD or, no, A CRY IN THE WILD but there are many other projects I'm working on. Films are limiting, though, and do not allow as much scope as books.

ptchestr: Do you regret not writing at a younger age?

paulsen: I only regret one thing in my life and that was about six years I tried drinking back in the Seventies. It was a complete waste of time. Well, maybe I regret parts of the army as well. I wish now that I had started to read younger, though.

ptchestr: Did anything inspire you to write books?

paulsen: I'm not sure if things did or not. I had a rough childhood, flunked out of school—I was what they now call a geek or nerd, the last guy chosen for sports, or not chosen at all, wrong clothes, bad grades all of that. Writing didn't come to me until I was almost twenty-seven, and then it took me, truly took me. After that I think it was my life, all of my life, that inspired me to write and to keep writing.

ptchestr: Why do they call you a "puffin person"?

paulsen: I have no idea. I don't look like a puffin. Or maybe I do, at that. A bald old puffin. I think it has something to do with marketing programs for Viking publishing.

ptchestr: We know you live in Minnesota, but what part exactly?

paulsen: I am writing right now from north central Minnesota. If you look on a map and find the town of Bemidji, I am about thirty-seven miles northwest of there, just out in the woods. My nearest neighbor is three miles away. Unless you count deer, bear and wolves.

ptchestr: In the book Canyons, why did you call the soldiers bluebellies? Is that what they were really called?

paulsen: That was about the kindest thing the Apaches called them. There were many other terms, none of which I can say here, but many of the different tribes called them bluebellies.

ptchestr: Why do you always write about boys and their adventures?

paulsen: Because I was a boy and had adventures. Most of what I write about happened to me and it's important to write about what you know.

ptchestr: What will the title of your next book be?

paulsen: I have a book coming out in June that is a sequel to Hatchet. It's called The River. And next fall I have a novel coming out titled The Monument.

ptchestr: Why do you always use crazy names for the animals in your books?

paulsen: I didn't think they were crazy—well, maybe so. I suppose because I am at heart crazy.

ptchestr: Why won't you write a mystery book? If you have, what is the name of the book?

paulsen: I used to write adult mysteries but have backed off on them. I have a series of books for young people starting next April called The Culpepper Books and they are mystery adventure books.

ptchestr: How come you write books with someone or something always dying in them?

paulsen: Actually I don't. Most of my books are about other things. But the ones you have read have those aspects. I have over a hundred and thirty books published over the years and many of them have no death or dying.

saccardi: What happened in your life that inspired you to write the stories, The Island and Canyons?

paulsen: The Island is about my son. When he was fourteen he had mental and physical islands he would go to and I tried to get him not to do it. I finally realized he was right and I was wrong and went to his islands with him. He is twenty now and going to be a school teacher soon and we are very close. Canyons came about because I was stationed in the desert in the army near Dog Canyon and found a skull with a bullet hole in the forehead. I reburied the skull in a safer place and left it. That happened back in 1958 but the memory hung there all the time until the book came.

saccardi: Have you ever had a dream like the one in The Night The White Deer Died? If not, where did you get the idea for the dream?

paulsen: I have had similar dreams; I had a dream where I watched men firing a mortar at me, over and over, saw them drop the shell in and saw it come up and curve towards me but it never came down. All those dreams, all the dreams that come from life or memories, come to all of us.

saccardi: Does the room in the Winter Room, Foxman, and Popcorn Days have any sort of connection?

paulsen: Yes, it was a real room. They used to sit and tell stories, the old timers, in that room. I still love to remember it, and the stories.

saccardi: Where did you first become a writer? What was the first book you wrote?

paulsen: I didn't start writing until I was twenty-six or seven, out in California. And the first book was Some Birds Don't Fly—a humorous look at the aerospace business, which I worked in before I was a writer. It sold four, maybe five copies. Total.

saccardi: Where do you get your names for your characters like Oogruk, in Dogsong, and Carl, in Dancing Carl.

paulsen: Oogruk is an Eskimo word that means bearded seal. I used it so some of my Eskimo friends wouldn't think I was writing about them. And Carl was his real name.

saccardi: In a few of your books you write about going back to the old ways like Dogsong and Popcorn days. Do you think that is something we should do? If so, how?

paulsen: No, I don't think we can go back. I think there was beauty there, and I will write more about the beauty, but we can't do things the old way any longer. We would starve. I read somewhere that if the trucks stop rolling into Boston the people would start starving to death in ten or twelve days. It's sad, though, when old and beautiful things have to end, isn't it?

saccardi: What's your favorite book that you wrote.

paulsen: My favorite book so far is probably Dogsong. I loved that book and miss writing it. But the best-selling book is Hatchet.

ptchestr: How many races were you in?

paulsen: I ran two Iditarods and fifteen or twenty other distance races varying between two hundred and five hundred miles. The Iditarod is 1,180 miles.

ptchestr: Why do you think that your first book wasn't that successful?

paulsen: Nobody knew my name and I don't think it was a very good book.

ptchestr: What was your childhood like?

paulsen: It was rough. My folks were drunks and all that meant—I didn't like much of it. School was a nightmare for me and my grades showed it. Sometimes I look back on my childhood as something I feel good about surviving.

ptchestr: Are you excited that one of your books is becoming a movie?

paulsen: Yes, in some ways. But there's a lot of work with it as well and sometimes the work can hide the excitement.

ptchestr: In your books you are very dramatic. Are you dramatic in real life?

paulsen: Ha . . . I don't know. My wife thinks so and I seem to get involved in pretty dramatic things—the Iditarod, sailing on the Pacific, etc.—but I don't think of it that way. I just live. God, I'd hate to get bored though, wouldn't you?

ptchestr: We would love for you to come to visit the Port Chester Middle School. Would you be able to?

paulsen: I've had to back off on school visiting—I'm sorry. But if I start up again I'll come on out.

ptchestr: Will you ever write a book about this project?

paulsen: I don't know—maybe. You do things, and they sink into your brain and then later they come up sometimes as books. Maybe.

saccardi: Can you still sail because of your heart?

paulsen: I think so. I think I could run dogs. Last winter in New Mexico I practically lived on a horse—I named him Harley. I had him in the canyon country where CANYONS took place and dragged him up and down cliffs, along with a packhorse, so I think I could sail.

saccardi: Do you ever read any Jack London? Because you both have the same style of writing.

paulsen: When I was a kid I read some of London. The problem with him is that he sometimes didn't know so much about what he wrote about. He didn't know anything about dogs, for instance, and that makes him hard to read now.

saccardi: How long a day do you spend reading? And how many dogs did you have in one of your teams?

paulsen: I read all the time. When I'm not writing, I'm reading. I read myself to sleep every night, read in the tub, on the toilet, I read while I was running dogs. A team can be up to twenty dogs but that gets a little crazy. I usually ran about fifteen and at the height of running races I had ninety-one dogs in our kennel.

saccardi: In The Voyage of the Frog, did you actually experience the part where David woke up and then the boat was covered with whale mucus?

paulsen: Yes. I had two sloops on the Pacific, one as a bachelor and one with my present wife. Everything in that book happened to me, including the whale snot—it is truly, truly rank. Smells like rotten fish and manure or something.

saccardi: What countries have you visited in pursuit of your writing?

paulsen: I have lived in Mexico, Canada, the Philippines and Alaska. No other countries. I do not pursue writing, I just live, and the writing comes.

saccardi: How did you get involved with Eskimos? What inspired you to write Dogsong?

paulsen: I spent time in Alaska training for the race, the Iditarod, and met Eskimos then and during the race. Dogsong came about because of experiences in the first Iditarod when I pulled into a village about midnight and a little kid came out and grabbed my lead dogs and asked me to teach him about dogs. I couldn't believe that an Eskimo kid on the Bering Sea would have to ask some white jerk from Minnesota how to run a team and that's when I started to think about the book. Right then. During the race.

A Reader-Response Workshop

Facilitating book discussion using reader-response techniques requires practice at every grade level. It can often be unsuccessful in early stages, before students become confident that the teacher is really interested in their responses and considers them valid. Because lack of success can discourage a teacher from taking a reader-response approach to teaching, it is important to think through what will work with your class and begin with enough structure to help students learn how to respond. Used badly, reader response is a rambling conversation; used well, it is a way to give students ownership of their own reading and the confidence to express their own ideas. The approach requires not only that the teacher prepare thoroughly, developing her own reading, but also that she anticipate the critical issues, nuances, and ambiguities that will lead to alternative readings. It is uncanny just how quickly students can detect that moment when the teacher falls back on "telling them what the work is really all about." Fearful of that moment, a teacher may instead avoid focusing the discussion at all. And that too is a mistake and a detriment to good reading. The issue is not whether the teacher should focus or structure, but how.

In conducting workshops on using reader response, we have used a set of ten principles for reader-response discussion leaders:

1. Provide students with opportunities to choose what to read.
2. Ensure participation by everyone in some kind of overt response.
3. Never take away control of a reading from the individual reader.
4. Believe in the possibility of every other reader's response.
5. Take time to engage with and savor the reading.
6. Read aloud and encourage others to do so.
7. Promote a spirit of openness and collaboration.
8. Insist on individual responsibility.
9. Avoid undue attention to error.
10. Do not insist on closure.

As we have demonstrated in Chapter 1, using novels by fine writers like Sue Ellen Bridgers and Gary Paulsen is a way of inspiring good book talk, both online and off. Another genre we have found effective for an online project, especially with high school or college students, is the short story. We often begin with one that can be read in only a few minutes during class, such as "The Story of an Hour," by Kate Chopin, or "Hills Like White Elephants," by Ernest Hemingway. *Sudden Fiction: American Short-Short Stories* is a useful collection of even shorter stories, as is its sequel, *Sudden Fiction International: Sixty Short-Short Stories.* Many other excellent short story collections are available, as well as yearly collections of contemporary stories, such as the *Pushcart Prize Stories,* the *O. Henry Prize Stories,* and the *Best American Short Stories.*

An exercise based on Kate Chopin's widely available "The Story of An Hour," which Christopher Renino has used in a high school classroom, Marilyn Jody has assigned in a college class, and both have employed in workshops for teachers, demonstrates some of the ways we apply reader-response techniques. The same approach and the same story have been used for computer conversations in Marilyn's online courses on the short story. We call this concept "kindling (not killing) critical response."

First, we ask students to read the story straight through, then to write a few sentences—without stopping to worry about grammar or how the writing sounds or looks. For journal responses outside of class, we suggest possible start-up phrases that are identifiably personal, such as "What struck me most was . . ."; "The feeling I had was . . ."; and "What bothered me (amazed, angered, etc.) was. . . ." Then we have the students share these thoughts with each other in pairs. With most classes or groups, the level of conversational "noise" tells just how effective this story starter has been for getting book talk underway.

We insist on letting students set the direction of the discussion, from their own questions and their own insights, even if that leads to a few false starts, as it will with some stories. Other approaches we use include asking students to identify and then share with a partner what they find to be the single most important word in the story; to write their choice of a discussion question and then exchange questions; or to identify their favorite part (or the most puzzling part, the most exciting, etc.) and then to read that passage aloud (or quote it on-screen).

When it does become appropriate for the teacher to offer questions, effectiveness is determined by the types of questions. They should be open-ended, encourage a multiplicity of responses, and further rather than end discussion. They should not be aimed at finding one "right" answer. That kind of information, when it exists, can be stated, not used as an oral test.

In order to focus without negating the discussion, you can prepare in advance by framing at least one question about each of the major aspects common to most stories: plot, character, setting, point of view, theme, tone, and symbolism. Answer your own questions to see how difficult it is to articulate an answer. Rephrase the question if it can be easily answered with a simple, one-word answer. Then examine the story from more than one potentially useful critical perspective (historical, biographical, psychological, archetypal, feminist, etc.). Decide what approaches raise the most useful interpretive issues for that story and your particular class. Develop at least one key question and one key comment that will raise these issues. (An example of this approach as used with the Chopin story appears below.)

The best questions are real ones that you and your students ask yourselves as you read and then ask each other when you talk about the story. These questions grow naturallly out of the story at every stage of the reading process—comprehension, interpretation, and evaluation. Start with them; they may be all you will need. Try to anticipate what questions your class will ask. What are they sure to notice? What might they miss? What will be confusing? Controversial? Questions that are likely to strike a responsive chord and engender discussion are ones that are specific to the story and to the class. Avoid questions that fish for *your* answer rather than probing for theirs; questions that leave the text behind ("What do you think you would do . . ."); questions that can be easily answered with a right or wrong answer ("Who told Mrs. Mallard that her husband had died?"); or questions that trivialize the story ("What is the husband's first name?").

Once the discussion is underway, there are intervention strategies that you can use to keep the discussion alive and lively. When students misread in matters of fact, suggest that they make sure of what is actually there in the text ("Let's look at that part of the story again"). When students disagree in matters of inference, encourage the difference and ask them to point to the passage, incident, etc., that the inference is based on ("Please show us the line, passage, incident where you got your idea"). When major issues do come up in the course of the discussion, ask students to read and discuss a passage you have chosen that will center on the issues raised ("This is a good point to stop and take a closer look at the story . . ."). When students are obviously achieving a significant sense of some aspect of the story, extend the response by asking others to jump in ("Margie, do you see it that way, or do you have a different idea?" "Tom, how do you see that?").

Validate all responses by acknowledging them in some way: in class, a nod, a smile, a word; online, brief and lively positive comments, directed by name, posted to the class bulletin board. Reinforce comments that lead deeper into the text ("Go on with that, Karen"). Restate to clarify but not to improve on or to change a student response ("Let me try to restate what you said . . ."). Summarize occasionally to help students make connections and recall the points that have been made. Rekindle the discussion by returning to the text. Read aloud, or have students do so, just for the pleasure of it. Enjoy the language, an amusing scene, a powerful passage, rather than forcing the whole discussion to be a matter of interpretation.

Choose language that allows you and your students to stay tentative. Use phrases like, "So far, what do you make of this . . ."; "At this point, what is your reading of this . . ."; or "What is likely to happen. . . ." Distinguish between fact and inference. Use phrases like "Based on what you know about the character, what might be the reason for . . ." or "From what you have read, what do you think . . . ?" Keep the text foremost by using sensory words like *notice, observe, hear, see*—"What did you notice about . . ." or "What did you hear when . . . ?" Guide and shape the discussion without steering it toward a predetermined outcome. The goal is to engender response and critical thinking, not to impose interpretation.

In talking about this phenomenon, we like to use the metaphor of learning to fly. A student pilot learns the hardest part of flying—landing—by practicing "touch-and-go landings." That means the pilot tells the tower she is going to "touch and go," she comes in for a landing, and, as soon as the plane is safely on the ground, she pushes the throttle and takes off again without ever coming to a full stop. We like to compare first, second, and all subsequent readings or interpretations of literature to "touch-and-go landings," with another flight always on the horizon.

The Story of an Hour
by Kate Chopin

Knowing that Mrs. Mallard was afflicted with a heart trouble, great care was taken to break to her as gently as possible the news of her husband's death.

It was her sister Josephine who told her, in broken sentences; veiled hints that revealed in half concealing. Her husband's friend Richards was there, too, near her. It was he who had been in the newspaper office when intelligence of the railroad disaster was received, with Brently Mallard's name leading the list of "killed." He had only taken the time to assure himself of its truth by a second telegram, and had hastened to forestall any less careful, less tender friend in bearing the sad message.

She did not hear the story as many women have heard the same, with a paralyzed inability to accept its significance. She wept at once, with sudden, wild abandonment, in her sister's arms. When the storm of grief had spent itself she went away to her room alone. She would have no one follow her.

There stood, facing the open window, a comfortable, roomy armchair. Into this she sank, pressed down by a physical exhaustion that haunted her body and seemed to reach into her soul.

She could see in the open square before her house the tops of trees that were all aquiver with the new spring life. The delicious breath of rain was in the air. In the street below a peddler was crying his wares. The notes of a distant song which someone was singing reached her faintly, and countless sparrows were twittering in the eaves.

There were patches of blue sky showing here and there through the clouds that had met and piled one above the other in the west facing her window.

She sat with her head thrown back upon the cushion of the chair, quite motionless, except when a sob came up into her throat and shook her, as a child who has cried itself to sleep continues to sob in its dreams.

She was young, with a fair, calm face, whose lines bespoke repression and even a certain strength. But now there was a dull stare in her eyes, whose gaze was fixed away off yonder on one of those patches of blue sky. It was not a glance of reflection, but rather indicated a suspension of intelligent thought.

There was something coming to her and she was waiting for it, fearfully. What was it? She did not know; it was too subtle and elusive to name. But she felt, creeping out of the sky, reaching toward her through the sounds, the scents, the color that filled the air.

Now her bosom rose and fell tumultuously. She was beginning to recognize this thing that was approaching to possess her, and she was striving to beat it back with her will—as powerless as her two white slender hands would have been.

When she abandoned herself a little whispered word escaped her slightly parted lips. She said it over and over under her breath: "free, free, free!" The vacant stare and the look of terror that had followed it went from her eyes. They stayed keen and bright. Her pulses beat fast, and the coursing blood warmed and relaxed every inch of her body.

She did not stop to ask if it were or were not a monstrous joy that held her. A clear and exalted perception enabled her to dismiss the suggestion as trivial.

She knew that she would weep again when she saw the kind, tender hands folded in death; the face that had never looked save with love upon her, fixed and gray and dead. But she saw beyond that bitter moment a long procession of years to come that would belong to her absolutely. And she opened and spread her arms out to them in welcome.

There would be no one to live for her during those coming years; she would live for herself. There would be no powerful will bending hers in that blind persistence with which men and women believe they have a right to impose a private will upon a fellow-creature. A kind intention or a cruel intention made the act seem no less a crime as she looked upon it in that brief moment of illumination.

And yet she had loved him—sometimes. Often she had not. What did it matter! What could love, the unsolved mystery, count for in the face of this possession of self-assertion which she suddenly recognized as the strongest impulse of her being!

"Free! Body and soul free!" she kept whispering.

Josephine was kneeling before the closed door with her lips to the keyhole, imploring admission. "Louise, open the door! I beg; open the door—you will make yourself ill. What are you doing, Louise? For heaven's sake open the door."

"Go away. I am not making myself ill." No; she was drinking in a very elixir of life through that open window.

Her fancy was running riot along those days ahead of her. Spring days, and summer days, and all sorts of days that would be her own. She breathed a quick prayer that life might be long. It was only yesterday she had thought with a shudder that life might be long.

She arose at length and opened the door to her sister's importunities. There was a feverish triumph in her eyes, and she carried herself unwittingly like a goddess of Victory. She clasped her sister's waist, and together they descended the stairs. Richards stood waiting for them at the bottom.

Someone was opening the front door with a latchkey. It was Brently Mallard who entered, a little travel-stained, composedly carrying his gripsack and umbrella. He had been far from the scene of accident, and did not even know there had been one. He stood amazed at Josephine's piercing cry; at Richards's quick motion to screen him from the view of his wife.

But Richards was too late.

When the doctors came they said she had died of heart disease—of joy that kills.

The Story of an Hour

ASPECTS:

Plot
Could the conflict raised by the story have been resolved in any way other than Mrs. Mallard's death? Is there more than one conflict?

Character

What kind of person is Mrs. Mallard? What words in the story best describe her?

Setting

What does the view from Mrs. Mallard's chair suggest about her response to the news of her husband's death?

Point of view

What reliable commentary does the storyteller provide that would not have been available if Mrs. Mallard herself had told the story?

Theme

What is revealed by Mrs. Mallard's "moment of illumination?" What is meant by "the joy that kills?"

Tone

What appears to be the attitude of the storyteller toward the events of the story? What words convey that tone?

Symbol

Do you see any significance in the references to springtime?

CRITICAL APPROACHES

Historical

The women's movement in the 1890s, when the story was written, was controversial. Women who protested restrictive marriage laws were seen as selfish and unnatural.

Biographical

Kate Chopin's husband died while she was relatively young, prior to the start of her career as a writer. Her father died in a train wreck when she was four years old.

Comparative

A number of her other works also depict women whose marriages are seen as repressive. Her major novel, *The Awakening,* also ends with the woman's death.

Psychological

The story of Mrs. Mallard might be viewed as a clinical study of repression.

Archetypal

Spring represents rebirth. Mrs. Mallard is seen as "a goddess of Victory," while the marriage is seen as a corruption of the natural order.

Feminist

Marriage is an institution that defines women in male terms. The male doctors totally misread Mrs. Mallard's "heart trouble."

ANTICIPATED CONTROVERSY (KEY QUESTION)

Is Mrs. Mallard selfish and unfeeling or the victim of marriage as a repressive institution that kills her by "breaking her heart"?

POSSIBLE AMBIGUITY (KEY COMMENT)

The author may be depicting love and marriage as a paradox for women, the "joy that kills," as reflected in the resolution of the story as death, not divorce or a redefining of marriage.

Computers in the Language Arts Curriculum

Computer Competencies and the Language Arts

Using the North Carolina model as an example of typical state requirements, it is possible to visualize a literature curriculum for kindergarten through high school (and beyond) that provides for progressive development of computer skills appropriate to grade level, to learning styles, and to the study of English, whether language or literature, reading or writing (see Tables 1–4 in this section).

In kindergarten, children can learn, if only from pictures, to identify the physical components of a computer system and the different kinds of computers in use at home or in the workplace. They can learn to recognize letters, numbers, and other keys on a keyboard. And they can learn proper care of the computer itself. At higher grade levels, these skills can be reinforced as new ones are added.

First graders can acquire basic computer vocabulary—words like *hardware, software, diskette, cursor, booting up*—and they can demonstrate

Table 1. Elementary Grades K–3. (Source: "Computer Skills, K–12." *North Carolina Standard Course of Study* [July 1992]: 45. Reprinted courtesy of the North Carolina Department of Public Instruction.)

	Societal Uses	Ethics	Terms and Operation	Curriculum Software Use	Keyboarding	Word Processing
Kindergarten	1.1. Identify the computer as a machine that helps people work and play.		2.1. Identify the physical components of a computer system (e.g., monitor, keyboard, disk drive, printer). 2.3. Demonstrate correct use of a computer.		2.2. On a keyboard, identify letters, numbers, and other commonly used keys (e.g., RETURN/ENTER, space bar).	
Grade 1	1.1. Identify uses of technology at home and at school.	1.2. Demonstrate respect for the computer work of others.	2.1. Identify the physical components of a computer system (e.g., monitor, keyboard, disk drive, printer). 2.2. Identify fundamental computer terms (e.g., disk, software, hardware, booting/ starting, cursor). 2.4. Demonstrate correct use of hardware and software.		2.3. On a keyboard, demonstrate the use of letter keys, number keys, and special keys (e.g., shift key, delete/ backspace, space bar, arrow keys).	
Grade 2	1.1. Identify uses of technology in the community.	1.2. Describe the right of an individual to ownership of his/her created computer work.	2.1. Identify the function of physical components of a computer system (e.g., monitor, keyboard, CPU, disk drive, printer). 2.6. Demonstrate correct use of hardware and software.		2.2. Locate and use symbol keys and special keys (e.g., period, question mark, Caps Lock, arrow keys, shift, ESC). 2.3. Demonstrate correct keyboarding posture and finger placement for the home row keys.	2.4. Identify word-processing terms (e.g., word processing, cursor, load, save, print). 2.5. Demonstrate beginning word-processing techniques of entering selected home row words, saving, printing, and retrieving text.
Grade 3	1.1. Identify the ways technology has changed the lives of people in communities.	1.2. Explain that the copyright law protects what a person or a company has created and placed on a diskette.	2.1. Identify the physical components of a computer system as either input, output, or processing devices. 2.5. Demonstrate correct use of hardware and software.	2.4. Use commercial software in content areas.	2.2. Demonstrate proper keyboarding techniques for keying all letters.	2.3. Use a word-processing program to load, enter, save, and print text.

Table 2. Grades 4–5. (Source: "Computer Skills, K–12." *North Carolina Standard Course of Study* [July 1992]: 46. Reprinted courtesy of the North Carolina Department of Public Instruction.)

	Societal Uses	Ethics	Curriculum Software Use	Keyboarding	Word Processing	Databases	Telecomputing
Grade 4	1.1. Identify the ways in which technology has changed the lives of people in North Carolina. 1.2. Identify computers as tools for accessing information.	1.3. State that violation of the copyright law is a crime.	2.5. Use commercial software in content areas.	2.1. Demonstrate proper keyboarding techniques for keying all letters.	2.2. Use a word-processing program to edit a paragraph and save changes. 2.3. Use a word-processing program to enter a paragraph into the computer and print it.	1.2. Identify computers as tools for accessing information. 2.4. Describe the difference between a print database and a computer database.	1.2. Identify computers as tools for accessing information.
Grade 5	1.1. Describe the influence of technology on life in the United States. 1.2. Identify computers as tools for accessing current information.	1.3. Describe the need for protection of software and hardware from vandalism.	2.6. Use commercial software in various subject areas.		2.1. Use a word-processing program to copy and move text. 3.1. Use a word-processing program to publish a report that contains centering, tabs, and more than one paragraph.	1.2. Identify computers as tools for accessing current information. 2.2. Identify database management terms (e.g., database, file, record, field/category, sort/arrange, select/ search, report). 2.3. Use a prepared database to enter and edit data.	1.2. Identify computers as tools for accessing current information. 2.4. Identify telecomputing terms (e.g., modem, upload, download, bulletin board, e-mail). 2.5. Compare the process of sending and receiving messages: electronically vs. nonelectronically (e.g., e-mail vs. U.S. mail, electronic bulletin board vs. classroom bulletin board). 3.2. Use telecomputing hardware and software to communicate with a distant computer or an online service.

Table 3. Grades 6–8. (Source: "Computer Skills, K–12." *North Carolina Standard Course of Study* [July 1992]: 47. Reprinted courtesy of the North Carolina Department of Public Instruction.)

	Societal Uses	Ethics	Word Processing	Databases	Spreadsheets	Telecomputing
Grade 6	1.1. Identify ways that telecomputing promotes a global community.	1.2. Identify examples of copyright law violations and possible penalties.	2.1. Identify the function of word-processing utilities (e.g., spell checker, electronic thesaurus, grammar checker, outliner).	3.1. Use a database to sort records. 3.2. Use a database to search for desired information given one criterion and given two criteria (using "and" or "or" connectors where necessary). 3.3. Use commercial software to organize and visually display data to draw conclusions.	2.2. Identify the difference between paper spreadsheets (e.g., gradebook, budget, sports statistics) and computer spreadsheets. 2.3. Identify spreadsheet terms (e.g., spreadsheet, column, row, cell, formula).	1.1. Identify ways that telecomputing promotes a global community. 3.4. Use telecomputing hardware and software to communicate with a distant computer or an online service.
Grade 7	1.1. Identify the role of technology in a variety of careers.	1.2. Identify, as intellectual property, work created using a computer. 1.3. Discriminate between ethical and unethical access to information stored on a computer system.	2.1. Identify terms related to computer–generated productions (e.g., desktop publishing, WYSIWYG, clip art, hypertext, multimedia, laserdisc, CD–ROM, VCR, scanners, camcorders). 2.2. Describe the advantages of using computers to generate various types of productions.	3.1. Given a prepared database, use sorting and searching techniques to solve a specific problem.	2.3. Use a prepared spreadsheet to enter and edit data and explain the results of the changes. 3.2. Enter and edit data into a prepared spreadsheet to test simple "What if?" statements.	3.3. Use telecomputing hardware and software to communicate with a distant computer or an online service.
Grade 8	1.1. Identify technological skills required for various careers.	1.2. Distinguish between different types of data as to which are public and which are private. 1.3. State the need for protection of software and hardware from computer viruses.	2.1. Revise word-processed text to be a simple desktop–published document.	3.1. Given a prepared database, use sorting and searching techniques to solve a specific problem.	3.2. Enter and edit data into a prepared spreadsheet to test simple "What if?" statements.	

Table 4. Grades 9–12. (Source: "Computer Skills, K–12." *North Carolina Standard Course of Study* [July 1992]:48. Reprinted courtesy of the North Carolina Department of Public Instruction.)

	Societal Uses	Curriculum Software Use
Grades 9–12	1.1. Identify examples and analyze the societal impact of advanced and emerging technologies.	3.1. Identify and independently use computer hardware and software for class and personal use.

keyboard skills, copying sight words by typing in the letters on a line below the words and "erasing" words or colors, using appropriate keys. They can learn how to handle a diskette, how to insert it into the computer, and how to press the keys and touch the unit without harm to themselves (it is, after all, powered by live current) or to the computer (no liquids, sand, or sticky fingers).

Second graders can begin to learn the ethics of creative ownership, respecting others' work on the screen and protecting their own. At this level, they can add more words to their computer vocabulary and can use more special function keys, such as the Caps Lock, arrow keys, shift key, question marks, periods, dollar signs. They can learn how to position their fingers correctly on the "home keys," how to save work on the screen, and how to print out their work.

By the third grade, children should know that it is wrong to copy others' work, whether from copyrighted software or classroom diskettes. They should be able to use keyboarding for entering all letters, know the names of the parts of the computer, and be able to load, enter, save, and print text. With this level of skill, they can use software in the content areas to practice many reading and writing skills.

At the next grade levels, students can learn about copyright laws for computers as well as for print materials. They should be editing their work by fourth grade, using a word-processing program to make changes, save them, and print out. They should be learning about print and computer databases, visiting the media center and seeing online catalogues, dictionaries, and encyclopedias in print and on CD-ROM. As they practice keyboarding skills, they can be using content-oriented software.

By fifth grade, their editing skills should include the ability to insert, place, and rearrange text. They can be using prepared databases to enter data. And they can become familiar with the terminology of telecomputing while observing the teacher using a network or while using it themselves, accessing current information from computer-accessible newspapers and communicating with other students via e-mail or bulletin board discussions.

By sixth grade, students could participate in an exchange of mail with students from another country; continue their development of editing skills using the spell checker, thesaurus, grammar checker, and outliner;

employ databases to search for information; and engage in research by communicating with a distant computer using an online service.

Middle school can be a time of rapid skill development in using computer technology, as students use clip art, hypertext, desktop-publishing programs, multimedia, scanners, camcorders, and other electronic paraphernalia of the technological world. They should be learning to differentiate between production terms like *text, video, graphics,* and *audio;* viewing and identifying computer-generated effects; and producing multimedia reports and productions. They should develop more advanced skills in the use of computer technologies to analyze, interpret, synthesize, apply, and communicate information in all areas across the curriculum. And they should be engaging in cooperative projects with other schools by means of online services.

In grades 9–12, students who have come through a curriculum like this one will be using computers for nearly everything—searching electronic sources; researching emerging technologies like voice recognition and virtual environments; using simulation software for problem-solving; operating desktop-publishing programs for school publications; exploring databases for research papers; and utilizing telecommunications equipment for exchanges of ideas with students and scholars around the world.

Student Research

A Simple Way to Integrate Technology into Your School

Randy Pitts

The most difficult part of this article for me was to find the gall to use the words *simple* and *technology* in the same title. Hardly a day passes when computer companies don't bombard us with a new upgrade, an enhanced version, or a mutation of their software package that, like a new antibiotic, promises it will cure all the unpleasant ills of computers and computer programs before them. Five years ago you had to have, according to companies like IBM, a computer with their new 286SX processor so you could do wonderful things with it. A few months later, it was the 386SX you just *had* to have, and then the 486SX. This year it's the Pentium PC. Now, they're starting to name them like cars.

I won't go easy on Apple either. They are just as responsible for this plethora of hardware and software confusion. First it was Apple II, then the II+, then the Macintosh, Centris, Quadra, etc., etc. Software companies are also involved in the upgrade fever. Take WordPerfect Corporation for instance. They have gone from WordPerfect version 1.0 to 2.0, then 3.0, 4.0, 5.0, 5.1, and the latest and greatest is version 6.0. (I will give WordPerfect one kudo: their new versions of software will at least use the files from the older versions.) Spreadsheets, databases, you name it, anything to do with computers changes faster than the average person can keep up with them. But you're not an average person: you are a teacher.

Teachers have even less time than the average person to keep up with this randomly changing technology. A teacher must learn something not only to his or her satisfactory understanding of it, but must then transpose it to a teachable process that can be shared with our students. If we had to change lesson plans every three or four months, would we have time to do anything else?

Let me use a phrase that you will hear often if you speak with people who try to sell you computer systems: "Let me be honest with you." The salespersons will say it, the technicians will say it, the delivery persons will say it. What they are really saying is, if you want to learn to swim, you've got to jump in, preferably to the tune of $2,000 or more per computer.

So, let me be honest with you, too: I'm cheap. With my financial leanings in mind, let's explore some alternatives to the hottest, newest, fastest, most expensive computer a salesperson can talk your computer department into purchasing. I mean, honestly, do you really need to have a CD-ROM drive in every computer in your school? Can you afford it? If you've got eight hundred children in your school, would you rather have twenty really technologically cool (translate that to *expensive*) machines that will do things faster than a speeding bullet and leap educational goals like Super-PC; and, of course, a line of students forty-long waiting for their turn. Or, would you opt for one hundred machines that, even though they won't say "Good morning, Annie or Joey" when a student logs on, will get the job done, and you've only got eight students vying for time to use each one?

Teachers will be responsible for teaching these requirements, more than likely in conjunction with their other subjects. With a class of twenty students, will it be more efficient to have twenty simple computers for them to work with the entire class period, or five of the super PCs that each student may be allotted fifteen minutes during the class period to use? (Not to mention the headaches of organizing, assigning, and directing that fifteen minutes of time.)

A simple computer system that will work today, yet grow with tomorrow—forbidden words! Money is typically the first forbidden word when it comes to computerizing a school. As wonderful as the changing face of technology is, there is a catch: each upgrade and each change costs more money and effectively puts the latest and greatest computers a little further out of the reach of educators. But do teachers really need the latest and greatest?

What Can You Do?

What follows is a suggestion on how to acquire a simple computer system that can be purchased inexpensively, or, and even better, how to acquire a simple computer system that uses, as its primary component, older computers that local businesses or universities may be willing to donate to your school. Each time the computer revolution moves a step forward, like a never-ending battle, a whole list of casualties in the form of outdated computers and software programs is left in its wake. However, these older computers are fine for simple tasks such as word processing, spreadsheets, databases, and communications terminals. And these are the skills that most states will require high school graduates to have.

An entire industry for the resale of used computers is in the making. IBM has a factory outlet division that sells "withdrawn and surplus" computers. A quick call to Apple revealed that they recommend a company called Sun Remarketing Systems that sells a variety of Apple hardware, new and used. Other large, reputable companies are getting in on the act, too. General Electric has recently started GE Remarketing Services and advertises "quality used computer equipment," including Apple, IBM, and IBM-compatible (DOS-based) systems. These companies offer new and/or refurbished used machines that are checked by technicians before they are resold and typically carry a standard 90-day parts and labor, 30-day, money-back guaranteed warranty.

IBM (or compatible) 286SX and PS1 computers are fine machines capable of doing all of the computer competencies required or soon to be required by most states. Apple's Macintosh Plus and Macintosh LC are also perfectly adequate computers that will also run the programs that fulfill required computer competencies.

What follows is a chart of average prices charged by these three companies as of April 1994 (you can be sure they will be lower by the time you read this):

General Electric Remarketing Systems had a refurbished IBM PS/2 Model 50Z, 1 megabyte of RAM, 30-megabyte hard drive, VGA color display, and 2400 baud modem. It comes with a 30-day warranty. Price $395.

GE also offers an Apple Macintosh LCII, with 4 megabytes of RAM, a 40-megabyte hard drive, but no monitor, at a price of $595.

IBM Factory Outlet had a new PS1, which is a 386SX processor, 2 megabytes of RAM, 85-megabyte hard drive, VGA color monitor, and a modem. It also included DOS and Windows™ installed, as well as Microsoft Works™ and Prodigy™. It comes with a one-year warranty, all for $679.

Sun Remarketing had plenty of used Macintosh Pluses with one megabyte of RAM, 20-megabyte hard drive, 9-inch monochrome screen (built-in), and modem. They included a 90-day parts and labor warranty and a 30-day money-back guarantee. Price $395.

Sun also offered an Apple Macintosh LCII, with 4 megabytes of RAM, 40-megabyte hard drive, and color monitor. Same warranties and a price of $895.

I am in no way recommending GE over Sun or IBM. The point is that so many older computers have been discontinued or discarded, a school can get a good price on them, a warranty, and deal with a reputable company as well. Call them and talk to them. They are in the business of selling computers, and if they can't help you, they will direct you to someone who can.

Let's take a moment to do some math. Using the previous figures, you can buy ten fully equipped IBM PS/2s for less than $4,000, and buying in quantity will more than likely result in an additional discount. Ten Macintosh Pluses will cost about the same. The Macintosh LCIIs and IBM 386s are a little more expensive, but five could be purchased for well under $3,000. The newest computers on the market easily cost $1,500 to $3,000 each, so would a school be better served by ten IBM PS/2s versus one Pentium? Or five Macintosh LCIIs versus one Quadra? Now multiply everything by ten and ask yourself the same question. If you are allotted $30,000 to purchase computers for your school, is it better to spend that money for ten of the newest, latest, and greatest, or seventy-five refurbished PS/2s or Macintosh Pluses, or thirty-three Macintosh LCIIs?

There is one thing you can be sure of, as I write this in May 1994: by the time you read it, prices will be much *lower*. A simple computer laboratory—whether IBM 286 or Apple Macintosh computers are used, whether they are bought or donated—needs to be tied into a network that is known as a LAN, or "local-area network." If we have twenty machines in a room, they can all share the same printer or printers by being networked together, so you don't have to buy twenty printers. A LAN works simply by plugging a card into each computer and then running a cable similar to a telephone wire from each cable to a central computer. The central computer then handles the "calls" from each individual computer and routes each "call" to the printer in the order it was received.

As of this writing, IBM or compatible printer networking equipment costs less than $50 per machine; Apple Macintosh LC networking equipment, less than $25 per machine. This type of concept will also work with a modem network so that the computers can call out to local or national online services to access the Internet or other educational communications systems.

Apple computers are even simpler to network than IBM. They have the software built right in, and it's only a matter of connecting the cable from the computers to the printer and a central modem. In this type of scenario, twenty students can have direct access to a computer for the entire class period, rather than having to share ten computers at thirty minutes each.

Software Considerations

Software packages have mutated through the same changes as hardware, but the end result has been simpler, easier to use, all-in-one programs that will do everything. Some of these packages are Clarisworks™, Microsoft Works™, and Lotus Works™. These offer simple word-processing, database, spreadsheet, and communication programs that will fulfill the average needs of any student.

When discussing software, a different type of network system may be recommended. In our previous printer network, the idea was to share a printer. In a computer network, the idea is to share software; however, that can be expensive and complicated, often requiring the school to hire or subcontract with someone who can manage the network. Why spend that money on another employee when it can be spent on more computers, software, or training?

With that in mind, each computer should have its own copy of the software package rather than having a network version that the computer users would all share. Why? It's simple (and cheap!). In a software network, if the main computer (fileserver) should have problems or need repair, the entire lab may have to shut down. If each computer can operate independently of the network, then in a worst-case scenario, where the fileserver is inoperable, the rest of the computers could still be used and the lab could remain open.

Individual systems also require less maintenance than a network and could be operated without having to hire or train someone extensively to run the network. Another advantage to this type of network is that, in the same way that each computer can share a central printer, each can also share a central modem or telephone line, used for telecommunications. Communications via the Internet or other networks is one of the hottest topics in education today. Graduating students will be required by most states to have a comfortable knowledge of it.

Whatever your requirements are, if your school has limited resources and a limited budget, used and refurbished systems can go a long way toward filling in the technology gap many schools face. The used and refurbished computer market will only grow larger as computers are replaced by more powerful and faster machines. The question teachers must step forward and ask is this: What do we really need?

Exercise in Memory: Three Hyperfictions

Howard Holden

The next paragraph might not make sense. Bear with me.

> He laughed, he was so old. They fanned out over the earth. In his turn he had two sons. He had no children, except one. He arrived later. A son was born. The brothers disagreed often. In his time, he had twelve sons. The younger one betrayed the older. He became the heir. He was illegitimate. God told him his children would number as the stars in the sky.

If you took a few minutes, you probably could rearrange it:

> God told him his children would number as the stars in the sky. He laughed, he was so old. He had no children, except one. He was illegitimate. He married later. A son was born. In his turn he had two sons. The brothers disagreed often. The younger one betrayed the older. He became the heir. In his time, he had twelve sons. They fanned out over the earth.

It is familiar now as the story of what many consider the beginning of civilization.

The first rendition is a random sorting of the second. Well, not exactly random; I purposefully left the tip-off sentence until last. I just wanted to present a story in an unfettered fashion, events not necessarily falling chronologically. I think you should know, however, that I wrote the second paragraph first.

Every author faces the same problem, which, at its essence, is how to present a related string of events in an interesting way. The variety of relationships of events might be endless, but there is one overriding and irrefutable relationship among all events: they happen within the confines of time. An event happens before, after, or at the same time as another. The order of that sequence—the narrative structure—lends meaning to the world the author creates.

Within that world, the author must construct time. Time has had its own effect on this, and as the body of literature has grown, event upon event, publication following publication, the construction of narrative has become increasingly challenging, and narratives have become increasingly sophisticated or messy—take your pick. In either case, the artistic challenge has become less a matter of what goes into the story and more a matter of how the story is told. Innovations in narrative technique may require readers to question their understanding of the world or at least to imagine a world in which time's properties follow different paths than the one we are used to, the one with which the reader is comfortable. And it is important to realize that in the Western tradition, time has had only one path— from the beginning until this moment.

Western narrative, for the most part, has mimicked this understanding of time. It has presented stories as strings of events, perhaps as cause-and-effect relationships, the first event causing the next. But, if we use the example of Abraham, we must see how it distinguishes human history from time. Abraham's progeny fanned out. History, rooted in time, branches event upon event. Still, if we look backwards and retrace the forked paths of events, everything eventually points to one. This method of presenting history, actual or mythological, has had no small effect on Western thought, philosophy, and religion, and points all the way back to a conception of an original event, caused by one god. Of crucial importance is the comfort this narrative tradition has offered Western societies by rooting the individual's existence in a continuum, linking her to the rest of humanity, and minimizing her isolation.

It is not always the artist's job to provide comfort, alas. More frequently, it is his job to stir up trouble, to force us from our easy chairs and ask, "Is this really the way it is?" Changes in narrative technique are one way of doing this, but even narrative technique has been confined, till now, to the linearity inherent in the physical structure of books. One deviation from chronological narration is the flashback. In *Wuthering Heights,* we enter the story in the middle, are carried to the beginning, then progress through to the end. We bring out of the book an understanding of the events in their chronological order, the narrative having served to pull in our interest. Yet, even if the story begins in the middle, we begin reading at the beginning of the book and progress word after word, sentence after sentence, chapter after chapter to the last word of the last sentence in the final chapter.

Without a doubt, books and linear narrative have had an effect on the way we think. The purpose of teaching classics in Western culture is to teach students how to think. One argument follows on another in a linear fashion, working finally toward a goal of knowledge, a truth, reached by reason and understandable to all. Some say our memory doesn't work that way, page after page. Instead, they say, it is associative, jumping from item to item. I remember the first moon walk, which reminds me of John F. Kennedy, which reminds me of my friend who lives in Dallas. Of course, we can think both ways—it is necessary that we do—and each individual has a capacity to think more effectively one way or the other. But, until this century, we stored knowledge and created fiction in a linear fashion because the technology of books dictated it. Then came computers. Then came computer memory. Then came hypertext. But not in that order.

On the simplest level, hypertext is the linking of separate but related pieces of information stored in a text format. Annotated footnotes are a predigital example. While they are not essential to the information in a document, they represent a link to pertinent sources and other information. The parenthetical expression ("see related story, page __") found in newspapers and magazines is another example of the hypertext concept. Hypertext, more than anything else, is the ideal that all the information ever assembled on a subject can be linked in smaller groups of text that an information gatherer can access at will and in the order that best suits her purposes. Given the massiveness of supply and demand of information, there is no more practical way for hypertext to exist other than on computers.

This presents new ways of approaching problems in reading, writing, thinking, and remembering:

> It is the organization of memory in the computer and in the mind that defines hypertext and makes it fundamentally different from conventional text. . . . Reading, in hypertext, is understood as a discontinuous or nonlinear process which, like thinking, is associative in nature, as opposed to the sequential process envisioned by conventional text. Associative thinking is more difficult to follow than linear thinking. Linear thinking specifies the

> steps it has taken; associative thinking is discontinuous—a series of jumps like the movements of the mind in creating metaphor. (Slatin 874)

Of course, Slatin is not using the term *metaphor* incidentally. It is no stretch to see hypertext, computer links, and machine memory as a great big brain. This similarity has not been lost on artists, and some fiction writers believe they have found the medium that will finally liberate the narrative from the confines of linearity. Hyperfiction, as the resultant genre is called, is a stretch.

Hyperfiction as a genre consists now mainly of novels. These novels, like conventional novels, have pages. These pages must be read on a computer, but the most important difference is that the pages of hypertext novels do not have numbers and that the order in which they are read is never the same. Usually, the reader may choose her own path through the novel. By the same token, the reader decides when she is finished with the novel.

Naturally, this produces new challenges and problems for both reader and writer, not the least of which arise from the medium itself—the fact that hyperfictions can only be read on the computer. That limits the readership to those with access to computers, raising questions of expense, computer literacy, and software. The hyperfiction I read came from Eastgate Systems of Watertown, Massachusetts, which has its own hypertext software called Storyspace™. Storyspace™ runs on either Windows™ or Macintosh platforms. This again increases the price of reading hyperfiction for the reader who has to purchase either platform. It also increases the likelihood of technical glitches and decreases the accessibility one more step. Accessing any form of hypertext requires a greater than average knowledge of computer systems. If you do not own a computer already running one of those platforms, it is probably more worthwhile to spend your time reading a conventional book. The hyperfictions are not yet refined as a genre, and there just aren't many out there. Still, they deserve our attention because their narrative potential is so unexplored. For those reasons, I will deal more with the hypertext linking systems than with the content.

In a *Washington Post Book World* review of hypertext, Richard Grant observes that

> Lacking a definitive, printed and bound form, hypertext pages are, in effect, lying around loose in the computer's memory. They can be connected in various, often quite complicated ways, so that reading a hypertext work becomes less like journeying from start to finish (tenuous concepts here) than like wandering around in a new environment. (8)

Achieving this wandering effect requires of hyperfiction writers some degree of skill as computer programmers.

In one of the first hyperfictions to emerge, *Its Name Was Penelope*, author Judy Malloy used a random-number generator to structure her story. A random-number generator is a program that picks a number with no regard to sequence. (Truthfully, they are called pseudo-random-number generators. It is impossible for a computer to generate a truly random number.) Whatever the first number is has no bearing on what the next number will be. Each block of text in *Penelope* is assigned a number and, as the random-number generator chooses, the corresponding blocks of text appear. To activate the generator—or turn the page—one just hits the return key.

Reading *Penelope* has been compared to sorting through a box of old, forgotten photographs. The photos, or text spaces, come to vision at random, each arousing unique feelings or memories with no regard for chronology. When the viewer has explored enough, he tosses the photo back into the box or sends the text space back to the computer's memory. The random-number generator should be a perfect mechanism for this, except that the person examining a box of photographs will set aside one when he encounters it for the second time. Following this pattern, he will most likely sort them until the box is empty. The photographs will then have some order that signifies something, and this is similar to what Malloy intended. The reader will arrange the story in some fashion significant to him in his own memory.

That goal is laudable if for no other reason than its own novelty. It certainly blazes a trail and raises another serious question about how we read. In one sense, the random-number generator fails because it has no means by which a reader can "discard" or "sort" a text space. Before a reader is sure he has seen all of the text spaces, he will encounter some over and over again, to the point of annoyance. In any material about or in hypertext, the question of when the reader is finished is present. The answer is always the same: it is up to the reader.

In his instructions to the reader at the beginning of *Afternoon, A Story,* Michael Joyce explains that this is a central issue to hyperfiction:

> Closure is, as in any fiction, a suspect quality, although here it is made manifest. When the story no longer progresses, or when it cycles, or when you tire of the paths, the experience of reading it ends. Even so, there are likely to be more opportunities than you think there are at first.

In a culture where book reviewers love to say, "He left me wanting more," this idea flies in the face of tradition. It is not what Western readers read for. Western readers, or at least Western scholars, read for something beyond the book. We want to be able to say what we got out of a book. In this way, our minds, when we are reading, are somewhere in the future, somewhere in the meaning we will take away, in the self-affirming linearity of sequential events, in the criticism we will write. Both Malloy and Joyce seem to be trying to bring our minds back to the experience of reading— the act of reading for no other sake than itself. Unlike Malloy's random-number generator, *Afternoon* has a linking structure that allows more choice than simply when to stop reading. A reader can page through in an order already programmed by Joyce, or she can "double click on certain words to follow other lines of the story. Window titles often confirm words which yield." The reader now becomes a player, which seems more true to the heart of hypertext. However,

> these are not versions, but the story itself in long lines. Otherwise, however, the center is all; Thoreau or Brer Rabbit—each preferred the bramble. I've discovered more there too, and the real interaction, if that is possible, is in pursuit of texture (in my mind). (Joyce n.p.)

One misconception about hyperfiction is that the reader helps create the story. This is true of interactive fiction, which can take place on computer networks, but as Joyce makes clear, there is only one version of the story. Slatin says "hypertext systems tend to envision three different types of readers: the reader, as browser, as user, or as co-author" (875). The browser wanders around a hyperdocument, enjoying items as they pop up. He quits reading when he wants to and is not really expected to read all of the document. It should be apparent that the browser is the reader most likely to enjoy the hyperfictions discussed here. Slatin's user has a specific goal or piece of information in mind and leaves the document when he finds what he needs. Typically, he is a researcher and deals with more factual hypertext material. Finally, the co-author contributes to the document as he browses through it or uses it (875).

The overly enthusiastic reader might purchase a hyperfiction with the hopes of co-authoring. There are a very few hyperfictions that allow this in some form, and certainly there are more to come. Neither *Afternoon* nor Stuart Moulthrop's *Victory Garden* should be mistaken as a narrative allowing co-authoring. When Joyce says that "real interaction, if that is possible, is in pursuit of texture. There we match minds," he expresses even his own doubts about interactivity. In an important contrast with Malloy, who leaves so much to the random-number generator, Joyce allows the reader more choice in experiencing *Afternoon*. In effect, *Afternoon* shares control between the writer and reader. The lion's share, however, remains with Joyce, who makes some links obvious and keeps some hidden. His invitation to pursue texture—he uses the word to describe words that yield—takes the experience a step further than Malloy. The browser is teased into becoming a user, manipulating the links to get at specific information. Joyce challenges us to untangle the web of narrative, to "match minds." But following this lead, we become prone to forget that the story remains under his control. "Using" hyperfiction leaves the reader vulnerable to being led around by the nose. I can hear the author laughing.

Stuart Moulthrop wrote *Victory Garden* on the same software that Joyce used for *Afternoon*. This accounts for most of the similarity in the linking system and the "look." As in *Afternoon,* the reader may "page through on a wave of returns," following a preprogrammed route laid down by the author. Or he may click on words which may yield to new threads. But while Joyce hides his yielding words, Moulthrop gives the reader the opportunity to highlight yielding words if he chooses. In addition, Moulthrop offers a map with various entry points into the story, along with other playful ways of entering. The browser has gained even more choice and is thus more susceptible to falling into the user category in search of that specific tidbit of "what happened?" Beware—Moulthrop isn't much nicer than Joyce about this. Moulthrop may also have realized that, in giving more choice, more linearity and chronology, he is producing a more marketable product. This points to some features that I believe may threaten the quality of future hyperfiction. Many people think hyperfiction grew out of computer games. This may have some small degree of truth, but it is only significant if we look forward instead of backward. Moulthrop's complex linking structure is more likely to intrigue the reader than the others because, as Coover says, it gives us the feeling of "a kind of obscure geography to be explored" (10), and as Mark Bernstein says, it is "playful." These are wonderful qualities in any fiction, and Moulthrop's artistic achievement is that he has used these qualities of the linking structure as a metaphor for a fractured society ruled on every level by the power, abuse, and unscrupulousness of mass media. But these qualities also make the genre uniquely susceptible to falling away from serious fiction into the world of computer and video games. (Bernstein disagrees with me on this point. Hyperfiction, he says, will flourish as long as someone has the urge to create it.) The exploding capabilities of CD-ROM carry this threat further as access to high resolution graphics and sound spur the development of hypermedia. As developments in software make it increasingly easy to include these sensory delights, serious hyperfiction writers will have to carefully weigh their value and predict to what degree graphics and sound will force text out of the work.

In a period when moving images and sound are increasingly becoming the way information and entertainment are presented and sold, this threat to text—to reading—is in danger of being underestimated. While hyperfiction writers strive to produce stories in a fashion that is different for each reader, we must remember that fiction has already done this since its inception. The difference occurs in the imagination, where the images and events are unique to the individual. The more that images are visually provided to the reader, the less that is required of the reader. As long as it is text based, hyperfiction gives us an unprecedented tool for stretching the reader's imagination. At their most profound levels, the linking structures reflect the increasing sense of an incongruous world. Events do not fall neatly into a linear history, and our tradition of imposing a linear order upon the nature of existence may express a desire to make sense of a chaotic world. If this is true, then Malloy's *Penelope* employs the most accurately reflective narrative structure. Randomness is the opposite of linearity. Of course, readers may not be ready for that extreme, and Joyce and Moulthrop have given progressively more choice to the reader, which, though it still results in a questioning discomfort, acknowledges that the reader is likely to reconstruct the story in the fashion to which she has been conditioned—that is, chronologically. Given the opportunity to choose her path, she will choose one she not only is interested in, but one she can understand and one that is not likely to go in a circle. Again, beware the pitfalls awaiting the "user" of hyperfiction. If you want to find Moulthrop in this story, he's the one who put the "welcome" mat at the door of this labyrinth.

Looking backward once again, what are we accustomed to reading for? Meaning? Connection to history and humanity? The truth? We drift somewhere between browser and user, wanting to take something away from the book by finishing the whole book, having to stop when we are tired, yet with the nagging sense that we have not read it all. That is the nature of these hyperfictions and their most significant contribution—to leave us as readers without support, chipping away at our existential base—the way we think that we think.

Works Cited

Bernstein, Mark. Telephone interviews. April 1994.

Bukatman, Scott. "Virtual Textuality." *Artforum* 32 (January 1994): np.

Coover, Robert. "Hyperfiction: Novels for the Computer." *The New York Times Book Review* 29 August 1993: 1, 8–10.

Edwards, Gavin. "Uncle John's Text: Talking with a Hypertext Novelist." *The Village Voice* 1 February 1994: 46.

Grant, Richard. "Beyond Books: Never the Same Text Twice." *Washington Post Book World* 11 July 1993: 8–9.

Joyce, Michael. *Afternoon, A Story.* For Macintosh or Windows™. Watertown, MA: Eastgate Systems, n.d.

Malloy, Judy. *Its Name Was Penelope.* For Macintosh or Windows™. Watertown, MA: Eastgate Systems, n.d.

Moulthrop, Stuart. *Victory Garden.* For Macintosh or Windows™. Watertown, MA: Eastgate Systems, n.d.

Slatin, John M. "Reading Hypertext: Order and Coherence in a New Medium." *College English* 52.8 (December 1990): 870–883.

How Literary Lists Are Changing the Way We Learn English and Literature

John Scott Kemp

As computers continue to work themselves into our daily lives, and, in particular, as they become an increasingly prominent and necessary tool within the educational disciplines, what seems imminent is that their ever-broadening application will bring about great changes in the field. Much has been written about the use of educational electronic networks, which Betty Bowen classifies as being of three varieties: "electronic bulletin boards, teleconferencing, . . . [and] electronic e-mail" (117). E-mail, like ordinary mail, is "essentially private, addressed to a single recipient or small group of recipients" (117), and during its premier decade, it has engendered a more specialized medium which is rapidly gaining votaries from every area of specific interest—the list. Lists, which are essentially electronic discussion groups, have been formed and are continuing to form rapidly every day for every conceivable special interest—from the traditional subjects of English literature or history, to those ranging from *Star Trek* to comic-book action heroes. Perhaps as important a reason for their proliferation is the relative ease with which a list can be set up and maintained. It requires (1) a host microcomputer upon which the list participants, or subscribers, from other sites can "post" their messages to be read by other subscribers; (2) a modem for conveying messages over telephone lines; (3) some special software, the kind which is largely available in the "shareware" format; and (4) someone who is willing to "own" or manage the list. The task of finding a list host is generally not difficult, as Allison S. Bartlett explains: "Managing a list is not all that different from editing a journal and takes about the same amount of time." This is further explained by Elizabeth Thomsen, a librarian who serves as the database manager for a multitype library consortium in the Boston area:

> I have been involved with the Internet for about a year. I sampled many different lists of all types. One that I stumbled upon was Austen-L, and I was fascinated by this ongoing discussion of a favorite author. Now I am the listowner of three literary lists of my own. One is Boston-book, a general discussion list for the Boston area. The other two are author lists—one on Anthony Trollope and one on E. F. Benson.

During the last few years, the general literary lists have further specialized into studies and discussions of individual authors and their works, for example, Milton, Shakespeare, Twain, and others. However prominent or obscure the authors are, a literary list can and will be organized, as long as a particular group of enthusiasts deems it a worthwhile endeavor. Although the effects of general telecomputing on education have been well scrutinized throughout a myriad of educational journals, published articles on the effect that literary lists have upon the discussion and, hence, the learning of English and literature, are difficult to come by.

As if to prove its own emerging puissance, the medium itself provides the solution to the problem of gathering information about this potentially important supplemental tool to the study of English by eliciting online interviews with the subscribers to the various literary lists, including students and professors, experts and novices alike. These interviews collectively reveal the trends that are guiding the use of "Lit lists" among English colleagues and demonstrate how the Lit list is changing the way we discuss and learn about English and literature.

Those who were interviewed comprise an exemplary cross section of the English/literature community that regularly uses Lit lists: Allison S. Bartlett, Ph.D. in medieval and Renaissance literature, professor at a small women's college in Washington, D.C.; Kenneth Nuckols, graduate student, teaching assistant in freshman composition, University of Central Florida; Christine Mack Gordon, assistant to the director of creative writing, University of Minnesota; Jason A. Pierce, American postgraduate student of Scottish literature, University of St. Andrews, St. Andrews, Scotland; Marilyn Jody, Ph.D. in English, professor at Western Carolina University and coordinator of the BookRead Project for WCU MicroNet; Nancy Miller, graduate student working on a Ph.D. in literature, Ohio State University; Elizabeth Thomsen, librarian, Boston, Massachusetts; and Lori Buhman, undergraduate English student, Evergreen University, Evergreen, Washington. What is remarkable about the information received from the eight interview participants is its complementary consistency, which serves to validate the communality of their experiences. Analyzing this data reveals some surprising trends, and despite the concerns of those few who view the Lit list as a threat to the classroom discussion group (contrary to the overwhelming opinion that it is a tremendous complementary tool to the face-to-face experience), the Lit list "posts" some definite and, in some cases, surprising advantages over the traditional classroom format.

Not so surprisingly, the Lit list provides its subscribers with the same types of benefits as those provided by traditional personal interaction among English colleagues. The following responses chronicle the ongoing telephone and telecomputer conversations I had with eight members of the English/literature community that uses Lit lists:

Jason Pierce: I use the Lit lists mainly as a hunting ground for ideas and as a means of communication with other members of my field who might be able to assist in matters of obscure references and rare source materials. In this way it is akin to the community of faculty and postgraduates at any given institution that would exchange ideas and knowledge. This particular community just happens to be larger and spread over an extremely large area.

Nancy Miller: I have just started my dissertation and am looking for Renaissance studies on the concept of chastity, and there doesn't seem to be any. I wanted to find if anybody knew of any recent work that I didn't have immediate access to, to supplement my own research. . . .

But far beyond these all-too-familiar benefits of collaboration, the split-second, electronic, wide-area nature of the Lit list affords some remarkable improvements. One of my first questions was to ask what they have gained from using the Lit list:

Allison Bartlett: Primarily, in my current situation, the list provides me with an academic community. . . since there are only three members in our English department here. . . . I also think that the potential for interacting with names on one's bookshelf is a wonderful opportunity.

Nancy Miller: It breaks down the isolation that one sometimes feels during literary research. You can sometimes "lurk" and eyeball discussions that are going on between rather well-known scholars, and between others not-so-well-known—it's nice feeling like you have a voice among people who may be names that you have read in journals, having easy access to the latest critical positions and ideas. . . .

Lori Buhman: Having people of higher caliber on the list, reading what they have posted, has enhanced my approach and understanding . . . rather than having to always look to the facilitator for the right answer. . . . The many ideas that I see when daily reading through the lists stimulates me into my own thinking more. . . . Sometimes as a voyeur to a list you will not actively be involved, but you will pick up all kinds of ideas. . . .

Christine Gordon: It's given me a great deal of pleasure in the context of other people [being] interested in the same subject . . . in an environment that feels very comfortable. I don't go look up anybody's credentials, so I don't know if I'm talking to a professor emeritus or an undergraduate. When I address the list I feel like we're all equal, and everybody is pretty much accepted as such. I enjoy hearing the conversations between all these people and allowing it to influence the way that I've been looking at different texts. . . .

What is clear from these comments is that the Lit list tends to provide a more experienced and mature forum for the discussion of literature, as its contributors—authors, professors, and students—participate alike. Such exposure is particularly beneficial for the students, who stand to glean the most in a medium which is arguably less "painful" than being "put on the spot" in the classroom discussion:

Allison Bartlett: I think the shier, particularly the more thoughtful, students, who may not be moved to announce their opinions in person, might feel far more comfortable articulating an opinion on screen.

Christine Gordon: The Lit list provides a nonthreatening place for students who are uncomfortable talking before a class, just as small-group discussion tends to bring out more participation than whole-class discussion.

Nancy Miller: I think there are "lurkers" out there who also lurk in the classroom. It allows you to let a little of your personality go out with your comments, you feel a little more palsy, like one of the gang. . . .

Kenneth Nuckols: I think it has helped us all. . . . It helps me to be a little more sure of myself. Another girl who has been very quiet, now, after a semester online, is more assertive in class, and I believe that part of that is due to the Lit list.

Christine Gordon: I know I'd feel intimidated if I heard one of these authorities present a paper at MLA or something like that, about going up to them and talking to them. But somehow, when they put up a question or comment on the list, and I have a response, I don't feel intimidated at all about giving that response—I think that's very healthy!

Not only do Lit lists build students' confidence and give them experience in a "nonthreatening" environment behind an "electronic veil" through which they can post their comments without inhibition, but they also allow students to see what is currently being thought:

Christine Gordon: It's a way to give students state-of-the-art information about what people in the field are thinking about. For example, a discussion that's currently [taking place] on the Shakespeare list [is] about how to interpret the last scene of *Macbeth*. That's wonderful to be able to bring something like that to students. And it's not something that was printed in last year's journal—its right now! It gives people the sense that this is all living stuff—it wasn't written twenty years ago, not dead material that sits in dry books on the library shelves and gets old. . . .

My next question—whether Lit lists are more productive or better in some ways than the classroom—brought about the realization of an exciting possibility: that the Lit list may actually be the improved hybrid of oral discussion and time-consuming written correspondence, as it combines the spontaneity and speed of the spoken exchange with the more polished and thoughtful statements and responses of written communication:

Allison Bartlett: I believe that academics are better writers than they are thinkers on their feet, that there's more lively discussion in this format . . . being able to think through a posting, rather than wishing to take words back. . . .

Nancy Miller: On a professional level, I would say yes, because I find that I write better than I speak. When you can sit down and compose, and do a little editing, and send it over the wire, I feel like it's going to be more polished.

Lori Buhman: The ability to go back and read over what people have said, the words are not lost, you can look for what they are really trying to say, then you have the time to ponder what you are going to say in return. . . .

Jason Pierce: The average posting to a literary list may not have the polish of a 10,000-word article, but the aim of both is the same—to disseminate information and to publicize opinions. Literary lists have the added bonus of allowing their subscribers to ask questions, making them potentially superior to any hard-copy literary journal that I am familiar with.

In addition to taking the best features from both the oral and written modes of literary discussion, by drawing from an international group of subscribers, the Lit list also brings a much broader base of knowledge to bear on any particular subject than would ever be possible in the local classroom discussion:

Lori Buhman: In the classroom environment, sometimes you are with a group of people when you go over a particular reading, and we don't really know the right questions to ask. On the list, though, because there are people on different levels, it really helps in guiding my thinking, bringing up all sorts of issues, which I'm afraid in the smaller groups might not be thought of.

Kenneth Nuckols: When you send one question out to the list and you have the possibility for interaction with thousands of others, as opposed to carrying on a discussion with one or two other colleagues face to face and all you have is their input (which tends to be limited since we are all so diversified)—that's quite an advantage. . . .

Nuckols further explains that one recurrent problem of the classroom—that of discussion becoming too specific or going off on tangents, at which time the professor must invariably redirect it—can be handled very effectively on the Lit list:

Kenneth Nuckols: Sometimes a general discussion will start off, and when it becomes very specific, it will go off-line between a few people, and when it is finished, someone will post the results of the discussion back on the list for others to get the highlights that came out of it.

The comments of a long-time advocate of computers in the study of English, Marilyn Jody, echo the resourcefulness of the Lit list as a significant mode of learning:

Marilyn Jody: My conviction is that using reader-response techniques and collaborative learning works enormously well with the network. A major advantage of using this approach to literary interpretation is that it validates everybody's personal reaction. The computer allows everyone to express [his or her] initial, personal responses to the literature, then to take that next critical step, exchanging ideas with other readers. Students begin to add to their own critical interpretation, see other points of view, and perhaps come to a community consensus about the multiple possibilities of what they've read—all without missing that first crucial validation.

Perhaps more significant is the long-term effect that the Lit list may have on the classroom format, as the students will now have the opportunity earlier on, via Lit-list exposure, to develop a broader base of literary knowledge and attain experience in discussing it, effectively cutting into the traditional monopoly of information and practical experience that the English professor has enjoyed previously:

Allison Bartlett: I believe that as we go farther into this, that [for the time being] our students are going to be far more active and far more knowledgeable about this sort of medium than the instructors are. . . .

Kenneth Nuckols: Some professors admit that they don't feel entirely comfortable with the new medium, although they are enthusiastic about this new resource, so that, though they have a definite edge over the student in the area of knowledge, they . . . feel that the student has an edge over them in their knowledge of the medium by which they're communicating.

Lori Buhman: Previously I'd only been involved in classrooms where the instructor had only one set idea and you needed to "parrot" that back on a test for him. When I joined the literary discussion groups and saw people "talking" about literature all the time, that really intrigued me: "Oh, people are really thinking about these things, you know, it's not necessarily down in stone where you need to go and find and dig through the tombs to find the exact answers."

Kenneth Nuckols: It gives me more confidence in talking about a subject if I've read some posts about it on the list. Undergraduates, especially, would feel a lot more comfortable putting a question on the Lit list than they would going to a professor's office. Some professors can still be dictatorial in the classroom, and it's nice if you can go to a source and ask a question, and there are so many different people at so many different levels of experience that are going to read that and be able to respond to it.

Marilyn Jody explains the balancing-out process that Lit-list involvement is liable to bring about in the future:

Marilyn Jody: I see excitement in the students, once the initial fear is over; I see excitement, and then a sense of power. When students feel empowered, the barriers between professors and students begin to soften and a sense of being learners together begins to emerge—with mutual respect a real possibility.

Not only the classroom format, but the nature of literary research in general is being transformed by the tendency of colleagues to be more "discipline-centric":

Marilyn Jody: The ability of specialists to connect almost immediately is an incredible asset. . . . The simple search for the information that I needed for my dissertation took two years to accomplish. Now I could probably accomplish the same task in a few weeks. The computer network can do much of the mechanical task in a hurry and allow researchers more time for thought and analysis.

Kenneth Nuckols: The Lit list gives academic scholars a superior channel through which they can exchange ideas. It makes communicating ideas easier, because you have the ability to compose a letter, get your thoughts together, send it out there, and get almost instantaneous feedback instead of having to publish a paper or article, or get together in conference.

Nancy Miller: I think the old patriarchal notion of one man forging ahead alone—that's going to break down and be replaced by more collaborative efforts, which are already taking place. There will be a new method of working—sharing of information—the idea of "if I keep you in the dark I can forge ahead" is going to go away.

Clearly, it would seem that Lit lists will promote a more interrelative, sharing literary community—not just on a local scale, but nationally and internationally—in which colleagues habitually turn to one another for almost instantaneous literary information, ideas, and solutions. Lit lists will foster a body of international colleagues that is more "discipline-centric," in which research projects will be less and less carried out by a lone person, but, more often, collectively by a group of researchers.

Perhaps the major impediment now holding back a complete proliferation of Lit lists is the lingering "computer phobia" that often plagues older, long-time educators, as well as some of their junior associates:

Allison Bartlett: There seems to be a few that are trying to drag the others kicking and screaming into the 21st century. [And] as long as administrations across the country deny electronic media [its place] in promotion and tenure considerations, [a place] I believe it should have, that mindset may be difficult to change. . . .

Christine Gordon: There are faculty here who are really gung-ho on it, and they're not necessarily the youngest faculty either. People are becoming excited about the new and different ways that you can use computers, lists, and e-mail, and all those kinds of things. . . . There are other people, [however,] who never look at their computer, except for word processing. Once most [of them] make that first step, the rest becomes easier. . . . It's a matter of persuading people that it can be done.

Lori Buhman: Here at our college, it came about because of the computer science faculty. . . . Some English faculty have never logged on and can see no reason why they should, and there are others who get a lot out of the Milton and Shakespeare lists.

Nancy Miller: A lot of the faculty are resisting—they may be close to retirement—but there are some who realize that they are going to be absolutely left behind without it, particularly when considering the competitiveness of the job market.

Invariably, all across the United States, there are still pioneering groups, and often single individuals, at every major university who are slowly convincing their administrations and other faculty members of their English departments of the absolute necessity of learning to utilize and harness the awesome power of the Lit list. One can only hope that the comments of Marilyn Jody, a literary-network pioneer herself in the Western North Carolina area, are prophetic:

Marilyn Jody: Right now everybody who is on a Lit list feels that they are on the cutting edge—and they are! But I'm not sure how long it will stay that way. . . . Eventually it will become the *in* thing to do and the "bandwagon effect" will kick in.

More extensive research with a larger study group in the area of how Lit lists will ultimately affect the way literature is learned will inevitably bring out perhaps never-before-realized ways of studying literature, as illustrated in these insightful comments by Jason Pierce:

Jason Pierce: People in different areas of the world invariably think differently. Before coming to Scotland, for instance, I was hopelessly unaware of the development of Scottish literature, [which] we Americans tend to lump under the term "British," sometimes being so unknowing as to mistakenly call it "English," something which the Scots find rather offensive. Imagine, then, the difference between a miniconference, for example, on Robert Louis Stevenson, being conducted at some northeastern American institution, versus one conducted via a literary list. The latter would allow for the input not only of people from Scotland, but also from England (where Stevenson's books were very popular), California (where he spent years traveling), Australia (where he spent some of his later life), and Hawaii (the nearest place with a university to the South Pacific island where he wrote many of his novels and short stories and where he eventually died). The total expense of travel alone for individuals from these sites would be staggering, yet through the Internet all can come together as a matter of everyday occurrence! I find that not only mind-blowing, but also heart-warming. The advantages for list users seem obvious: vastly expanded access to information, vastly expanded routes of communication, and vastly expanded connections with peers and colleagues all over the world! I cannot see any graduate student or faculty member worth his or her salt being able to exist without access to such lists in a decade's time.

Such a wealth of optimistic speculation cannot help but lead back to perhaps the most intriguing and controversial question generated by this remarkable new literary resource: Will the Lit list of today become the classroom of the future? Responses to this line of inquiry were more reserved as to the ultimate fate of the Lit list as a would-be "electronic messiah":

Christine Gordon: I don't think so. . . . It's not going to eclipse the classroom experience because there's nothing quite as amazing as that face-to-face interchange. I think it's going to complement it in really interesting ways, especially as more and more people get online.

Nancy Miller: The Lit list will remain a tool—a supplement—so that instead of anything replacing anything else, there will be a lot more integration of different techniques—at least I hope that will be the way it goes.

Kenneth Nuckols: I don't think it will replace the classroom but will only enhance it. Scholarship will pass us a lot more immediately than it used to.

Allison Bartlett: I feel that most of those who oppose the integration of the Lit list into the literary education process actually feel threatened by the electronic medium itself [the computer]. I don't see the Lit list taking the place of the classroom. I see it augmenting what occurs there, both for the instructor and the student. I don't know if it can replace the classroom any more than the electronic text can replace the printed book. It's a wonderful way to augment the classroom, a wonderful way to speed up research, discussion, and communication—but it's not going to replace them.

Yet, given the advancements of computer and communications technologies and the miraculous virtual realities that now seem to loom on the horizon, and remembering a time when most held the first "talking" movies and television as "passing fancies," one must not be afraid to grant the capacity of the Lit list to fulfill roles in the future that today seem slight. As Jason Pierce puts it:

Jason Pierce: Although the power of the Lit list can be awe-inspiring, it is still far from perfect. E-mail postings may be able to traverse continents in minutes, but they will never be able to replace basic face-to-face conversations. But I'm not saying that such will not be the case in the future, however. The Internet is expanding so rapidly that I can easily envision videophones and video e-mail coming into everyday use long before I think about retiring.

Perhaps, then, open-mindedness, when considering the future use of the literary list and telecomputing in general, is the safest, most realistic, and awe-inspiring approach, as summed up in the comments of Marilyn Jody:

Marilyn Jody: I'm convinced that we have to think in new ways about what computers are going to mean in a world we can't yet fully imagine. I think they will be tools, as books have been, that we can use to keep stories in our lives. Humans have always had storytelling as a way of seeking and of preserving what the community saw as truth. If the computer makes it possible to go on telling stories in newer and better ways, that is what we will do with them, inevitably. Books might be replaced, and computers too, but not stories. Without stories, our species won't survive.

Works Cited

Bartlett, Allison S. Telephone interview. 7 March 1994.

Bowen, Betsy A. "Telecommunications Networks: Expanding the Contexts for Literacy." *Literacy and Computers: The Complications of Teaching and Learning with Technology.* Ed. Cynthia L. Selfe and Susan Hilligoss. New York: MLA, 1994. 113–29.

Buhman, Lori. Telephone interview. 7 March 1994.

Gordon, Christine Mack. Telephone interview. 11 March 1994.

Jody, Marilyn. Personal interview. 30 March 1994.

Miller, Nancy. Telephone interview. 7 March 1994.

Nuckols, Kenneth. Telephone interview. 6 March 1994.

Pierce, Jason A. Internet e-mail interview. 4 April 1994.

Thomsen, Elizabeth. Internet e-mail interview. 5 April 1994.

Bibliography

Works Cited

Antonucci, Ron. "Rylant on Writing." *School Library Journal* 39 (1993): 26–29.

Aronson, Marc. "It Starts with a Word." *School Library Journal* 43 (1997): 30–32.

Bankhead, Betty. "Through the Technology Maze: Putting the CD-ROM to Work." *School Library Journal* 37 (1991): 44–49.

Bellow, Saul. Editorial. *New York Times* (10 March 1994): A25.

"BookRead." Online Project. Cullowhee, NC: Western Carolina University, WCU MicroNet, 1990–1994.

Boyer, Ernest L. "Shaping the Future: A Five-Point Plan for Education Reform." *Electronic Learning* 12 (1992): 66.

Chopin, Kate. "The Story of an Hour." *The Complete Works of Kate Chopin.* Vol. I. Baton Rouge: Louisiana State University Press, 1969. 352–54.

Computer Competencies for All Educators in North Carolina Public Schools. Raleigh, NC: Department of Public Instruction, 1992.

Coover, Robert. "Hyperfiction: Novels for the Computer." *New York Times Book Review* (29 August 1993): 1, 8–10.

Dreyfus, Hubert L. "What Computers Still Can't Do." *The Key Reporter* 59.2 (Winter 1993–94): 4–9.

Giblin, James Cross. Address. Children's Literature Conference, Teacher's College, Columbia University. New York, 8 May, 1989.

Hancock, Vicki, and Frank Betts. "From the Lagging to the Leading Edge." *Educational Leadership* 51 (1994): 24–29ff.

Holden, Howard. "Exercise in Memory: Three Hyperfictions." Unpublished paper. Cullowhee, NC: Western Carolina University, 1994.

_____. "Turning the Page: Reading in the DEM." Unpublished paper. Cullowhee, NC: Western Carolina University, 1994.

Jones, Sue, ed. "The Key Elements of Effective State Planning for Educational Technology." Atlanta: Southern Regional Education Board (SREB), 1993.

Kemp, John Scott. "How Literary Lists Are Changing the Way We Learn English and Literature." Unpublished paper. Cullowhee, NC: Western Carolina University, 1994.

Leu, Donald J., Jr., ed. "Exploring Literacy on the Internet." *The Reading Teacher* 51. 1 (September 1997).

Mazer, Norma Fox. "The Ice Cream Syndrome (AKA Promoting Good Reading Habits)". In *Authors' Insights: Turning Teenagers into Readers and Writers,* ed. Donald R. Gallo. Portsmouth, NH: Boynton/Cook, 1992. 21–31.

North Carolina Standard Course of Study. "Computer Skills, K–12." Raleigh, NC: Dept. of Public Instruction, State Board of Education, July 1992.

Peck, Richard. "Nobody But a Reader Ever Became a Writer." In *Authors' Insights: Turning Teenagers into Readers and Writers,* ed. Donald R. Gallo. Portsmouth, NH: Boynton/Cook, 1992. 79–89.

Pitts, Randy. "A Simple Way to Integrate Technology Into Your School." Unpublished paper. Cullowhee, NC: Western Carolina University, 1994.

Selfe, Cynthia, and Susan Hilligoss, eds. *Literacy and Computers: The Complications of Teaching and Learning With Technology.* New York: MLA, 1994.

Stinson, Joseph. "Reinventing High School." *Electronic Learning* 13 (1994: 23).

Williams, Debbie J. "Teaching with Technology or the Technology of Teaching: Reconstructing Authority in the Classroom." *The ACE Journal* 1 (1997): 41–49.

Children's Books

Aardema, Verna. *A Bookworm Who Hatched.* Photos Dede Smith. Katonah, NY: Owen, 1993.
Folktale reteller Verna Aardema writes about how her first poem, written at age eleven, launched her writing career.

The African American Experience: A History on CD-ROM. Minneapolis, MN: Quanta, 1993.
Covering prehistory through the twentieth century, this electronic database presents the history of African Americans from their African roots to their migration to the United States. Includes biographies and pictures.

Alcott, Louisa May. *Little Women.* New York: Grosset & Dunlap, 1987.
The delightful story of four girls growing up in New England during the Civil War. CD-ROM version available.

The American Indian: A Multimedia Encyclopedia, New York: Facts on File, 1993.
This CD-ROM database contains information on the history of North American tribes and leaders including stories and legends from more than sixty tribes.

Animals and How They Grow. Washington, DC: National Geographic, 1993.
Five CD-ROM-based picture books about the development of mammals, birds, reptiles, amphibians, and insects.

Avi. *Who Was That Masked Man, Anyway?* New York: Orchard, 1992.
Enamored with radio adventure programs, Frankie involves his best friend, Mario, in a plot to prove that the family boarder, a medical student who keeps a skeleton in his closet, is an evil scientist. This story is told only in dialogue and is hilarious!

Ballard, Robert. *Exploring the Titanic.* Illus. Ken Marschall. New York: Scholastic, 1988.
Describes the sinking of the luxury liner in 1912 and the discovery and exploration of the underwater wreckage. Available as an electronic book.

Belton, Sandra. *From Miss Ida's Porch*. Illus. Floyd Cooper. New York: Four Winds, 1993.
Neighborhood residents love to gather on Miss Ida's porch in the evening to share stories about past events of significance to them as African Americans.

Berger, Barbara. *Grandfather Twilight*. New York: Philomel, 1984.
Carrying a pearl aloft, Grandfather Twilight walks to the edge of the forest at the end of the day and launches the pearl into the night sky.

Bernhard, Emery, and Durga Bernhard. *A Ride on Mother's Back: A Day of Baby Carrying Around the World*. San Diego: Harcourt Brace, 1996.
The authors describe how mothers of different cultures carry their babies.

The Bookman Merriam-Webster Collegiate Dictionary, Speaking Edition. Burlington, NJ: Franklin Electronic Publishers, 1996.
A CD-ROM that contains the entire dictionary, a thesaurus and grammar guide, spelling corrections, and a subject search feature.

Bridgers, Sue Ellen. *Notes for Another Life*. New York: Knopf, 1981.
Because his father is mentally ill, sixteen-year-old Kevin fears he is afflicted with the same sickness.

_____. *Permanent Connections*. New York: Harper, 1987.
Rob, who has been difficult and often in trouble, is forced by his father to spend the summer working on his injured uncle's farm.

Brown, Marc. *Arthur's Reading Race*. New York: Random House, 1996.
Little D. W. claims she can read and proves it by reading ten signs found in the environment. An electronic book.

———. *Arthur's Birthday*. Boston: Little Brown, 1989.
A conflict arises when Muffy schedules her birthday party at the same time as Arthur's, but Arthur comes up with a plan to solve the problem. Available in English and Spanish, and as an electronic book.

———. *Arthur's Teacher Trouble*. Boston: Little Brown, 1986.
Arthur's third-grade teacher is the strictest teacher in the school. And to add to his miseries, Arthur must represent his class in a spellathon. Available in English and Spanish. Available as an electronic book.

Bunting, Eve. *Once Upon a Time.* Photos John Pezaris. Katonah, NY: Owen, 1995.
Bunting talks about her childhood in her native Ireland, her emigration to the United States, and her life as a writer.

Byars, Betsy. *The Moon and I.* Englewood Cliffs, NJ: J. Messner, 1991.
While recounting her humorous adventures with a snake she names Moon, Byars tells the reader a good deal about her life and writing. A very valuable book.

Cannon, Janelle. *Stellaluna.* Novato, CA: Broderbund/Living Books/Random House, 1996.
When a small fruit bat is separated from her mother, a family of birds temporarily takes her in. An electronic book.

Carlstrom, Nancy White. *Raven and River.* Illus. Jon Van Zyle. Boston: Little Brown, 1997.
Arctic animals plead with the river to wake up from its long icy sleep.

Cleary, Beverly. *A Girl from Yamhill: A Memoir.* New York: Morrow, 1988.
Cleary writes engagingly about her childhood years and her growing interest in writing. A must for those who cut their reading teeth on Cleary's books.

_____. *My Own Two Feet: A Memoir.* New York: Morrow, 1995.
The author continues the story of her life in this sequel to *A Girl from Yamhill.*

Cowan, Catherine. *My Life with the Wave.* Based on the story by Octavio Paz. Illus. Mark Buehner. New York: Lothrop, 1997
A young boy becomes so fond of a wave during a family vacation at the beach that he convinces his parents to allow him to take the wave home with him.

DeFelice, Cynthia. *Weasel.* New York: Macmillan, 1990.
In the frontier wilderness of 1839, Nathan and his sister learn that their father has been injured because of the Indian killer, Weasel. Nathan comes to terms with his hatred of Weasel and his desire for revenge.

Dr. Seuss. *Dr. Seuss's ABC.* New York: Random, 1963.
Humorous verses and many different words are given for each letter of the alphabet. Available as an electronic book.

_____. *The Cat in the Hat.* Novato, CA: Broderbund/Random House, 1997.
When two children are home alone on a rainy day, a naughty cat pays them a visit and wreaks havoc in the house. A CD-ROM.

_____. *Green Eggs and Ham.* Novato, CA: Broderbund/Random House, 1996.
Sam-I-Am repeatedly tries to persuade his friend that green eggs and ham are a tasty treat. An electronic book. A CD-ROM.

Edwards, Pamela Duncan. *Some Smug Slug.* Illus. Henry Cole. New York: Harper-Collins, 1996.
A slug, ignoring the warnings of those around him, meets a sad end. This story takes the "s" sound to new heights!

Esbensen, Barbara Juster. *Dance with Me.* Illus. Megan Lloyd. New York: HarperCollins, 1995.
A collection of poems describing the many dances in which nature engages.

Esterl, Arnica. *Okino and the Whales.* Illus. Mark Zawadzki. San Diego: Harcourt, 1995.
A mother tells her young child the story of a woman who rescues her daughter from the underwater home of the whales.

Fritz, Jean. *Homesick: My Own Story.* Illus. by Margot Tomes. New York: Putnam, 1982.
Although all the events are true, Fritz has fictionalized this account of her childhood years in China.

———. *Surprising Myself.* Photos Andrea Fritz Pfleger. Katonah, NY: Owen, 1992.
Fritz writes about her life as an adventurer who often finds surprises which weave their way into her stories.

Garland, Sherry. *Shadow of the Dragon.* New York: Harcourt, 1993.
High school sophomore Danny Vo tries to resolve the conflict betwen the values of his Vietnamese refugee family and the American way of life. Garland has several fine books that deal with the Vietnamese culture.

George, Jean Craighead. *Cry of the Crow.* New York: Harper, 1980.
While caring for a crow, Mandy learns a great deal about herself and her family.

_____. *Gull Number 737.* New York: Crowell, 1964.
After five summers of observing gulls with his ornithologist father, Luke begins to resent his father's autocratic attitude and longs to pursue some ideas of his own.

_____. *Julie of the Wolves.* New York: Harper, 1972.
A young Eskimo girl is saved from death in the wilderness by convincing a pack of wolves to care for her as one of their own.

———. *Julie.* Illus. Wendell Minor. New York: HarperCollins, 1994.
In this sequel to *Julie of the Wolves,* an older Julie returns to her father's village and struggles to save her Arctic wolves.

_____. *The Moon of the Alligators.* Illus. Michael Rothman. New York: Harper, 1991.
An alligator tries to survive in the Florida Everglades during the month of October.

_____. *The Moon of the Salamanders.* Illus. Marlene H. Werner. New York: Harper, 1992.
A male salamander goes to the pond to choose a mate. Beautiful illustrated account of this species' mating and birthing process.

_____. *One Day in the Alpine Tundra.* Illus. Walter Gaffney-Kessell. New York: Crowell, 1984.
Alone in the alpine tundra on a stormy day, a young boy goes adventuring.

_____. *One Day in the Desert.* Illus. Fred Brenner. New York: Crowell, 1983.
The Author demonstrates how the animal and human inhabitants of the Sonoran Desert in Arizona adapt to survive the desert's unrelenting heat.

_____. *One Day in the Prairie.* Illus. Bob Marstall. New York: Crowell, 1986.
The animals in a wildlife refuge on the prairie seek shelter from an oncoming tornado.

_____. *One Day in the Woods.* Illus. Gary Allen. New York:Crowell, 1988.
Animal and plant life in the Teatown Woods of New York as seen through the eyes of a young girl.

_____. *Shark Beneath the Reef.* New York: Harper, 1989.
A young Mexican boy comes of age as he becomes aware of the politics and corruption surrounding him. Wonderful glimpse into life in a small Mexican fishing village.

_____. *Water Sky.* New York: Harper, 1987.
An adolescent boy leaves his home in Maine to live in Alaska with his father for awhile. There he learns something about his roots and the importance of whales in Eskimo culture.

Ghazi, Suhaib Hamid. *Ramadan.* Illus. Omar Rayyan. New York: Holiday House, 1996.
Ghazi describes the celebration of the month of Ramadan and its significance in the Islamic religion.

Gibbons, Gail. *Whales.* New York: Holiday House, 1991.
The author describes different kinds of whales and the importance of protecting these giant creatures of the sea.

Giblin, James Cross. *Be Seated: A Book About Chairs.* New York: Harper, 1993.
Chronicles the significance of chairs from prehistory to the present. Includes a bibliography.

_____. *Let There Be Light: A Book About Windows.* New York: Crowell, 1988.
The author chronicles the development of windows from prehistory to the present day. Includes a bibliography.

_____. *The Riddle of the Rosetta Stone: Key to Ancient Egypt.* New York: Crowell, 1990.
Giblin describes how the discovery of the Rosetta Stone unlocked the secret of Egyptian hieroglyphics. Includes a bibliography.

_____. *The Truth About Santa Claus.* New York: Crowell, 1985.
Giblin explains where our idea of Santa Claus comes from. Includes a bibliography.

Goble, Paul. *Hau Kola = Hello Friend.* Photos. Gerry Perrin. Katonah, NY: Owen, 1994.
Author Paul Goble writes about how his love of all things Indian, even as a child, led him to write and paint pictures about native peoples and their myths and legends.

Greenfield, Eloise, and Lessie J. Little. *Childtimes: A Three-Generation Memoir.* New York: Harper Trophy, 1993.
Greenfield and her mother team up to tell this touching memoir, which spans three generations.

Grolier Multimedia Encyclopedia 1998. Danbury, CT: Grolier, 1998.
Provides 36,000 articles and extensive Web links.

Hallworth, Grace, comp. *Down by the River: Afro-Caribeban Rhymes, Games, and Songs for Children.* Illus. Caroline Binch. New York: Scholastic, 1996.
A collection of poems and chants from the Caribbean.

Henkes, Kevin. *Lilly's Purple Plastic Purse.* New York: Greenwillow, 1996.
When Lilly's teacher refuses to allow her to show her purse in class, Lilly gets even, only to regret her actions later.

_____. *Sheila Rae, the Brave.* New York: Greenwillow, 1987.
Although she is not afraid of anything, Sheila Rae must rely on her younger sister Louise to get them home safely when they become lost. An electronic book.

Ho, Minfong. *Maples in the Mist: Children's Poems from the Tang Dynasty.* Illus. Jean Tseng and Mou-sien Tseng. New York: Lothrop, 1996.
A collection of simple Chinese poems traditionally taught to children. Lovely illustrations.

Hoberman, Mary Ann. *My Song is Beautiful.* Boston: Little Brown, 1994.
Fourteen poems written in first person by different authors. Illustrated by different artists, each poem celebrates a unique culture and heritage.

Hopkins, Lee Bennett. *The Writing Bug.* Photos. Diane Rubinger. Katonah, NY: Owen, 1993.
Author Lee Bennett Hopkins writes about how he began his career as a teacher, began writing articles for picture books, and eventually shifted to writing novels, picture books, and poetry.

Howe, James. *Playing with Words.* Photos. Michael Craine. Katonah: NY: Owen, 1994.
Author Howe writes about his daily routine as a writer, the source of his popular "Pinky and Rex" series, and his love of words.

Hoyt-Goldsmith, Diane. *Celebrating Hanukkah.* Photos Lawrence Migdale. New York: Holiday House, 1996.
A Jewish family living in San Francisco celebrates Hanukkah. Presents the history and significance of this holiday.

The Human Body. Washington, DC: National Geographic, 1944.
This CD-ROM provides a fascinating look at the human body and includes information about the skeleton, the digestive system, muscles, the nervous system, and reproduction.

Hyman, Trina Schart. *Self-Portrait: Trina Schart Hyman.* Reading, MA: Addison-Wesley, 1981.
Hyman writes about her life and her art.

Johnston, Tony. *Day of the Dead.* Illus. Jeanette Winter. San Diego: Harcourt Brace & Co., 1997.
Johnston describes how a Mexican family celebrates the Day of the Dead.

_____. *How Many Miles to Jacksonville?* Illus. Bart Forbes. New York: Putnam, 1996.
A memoir of life in Jacksonville, Texas, in the first half of the twentieth century.

_____. *Whale Song: A Celebration of Counting.* Illus. Ed Young. New York: Putnam, 1987.
Whale songs are used to illustrate the numbers from one to ten in this counting book.

King, Elizabeth. *Chile Fever: A Celebration of Peppers.* New York: Dutton, 1995.
Beautiful photos and words describe the glories of various kinds of chiles.

Kuskin, Karla. *Thoughts, Pictures, and Words.* Photos Nicholas Kuskin. Katonah, NY: Owen, 1995.
Kuskin talks about her writing life in Brooklyn, New York, and where she gets the ideas for her poems and stories.

Lauber, Patricia. *Great Whales: The Gentle Giants.* Illus. Pieter Folkens. New York: Holt, 1991.
The author discusses various behaviors of different kinds of whales and why they are threatened with extinction.

Lee, Milly. *Nim and the War Effort.* Illus. Yangsook Choi. New York: Farrar Straus & Giroux, 1997.
A Chinese American girl living in San Francisco during World War II tries desperately to win a paper collection drive to help the war effort.

Lesser, Carolyn. *Storm on the Desert.* Illus. Ted Rand. San Diego: Harcourt, 1997.
  In lyrical language, the author describes a storm on an Arizona desert.

Lester, Helen. *Author: A True Story.* Boston: Houghton Mifflin, 1997.
  With wry humor, the author describes how she succeeded in becoming a published author, despite being a mirror-writer.

Levine, Ellen. *If Your Name Was Changed at Ellis Island.* Illus. Wayne Parmenter. New York: Scholastic, 1994.
  In question-and-answer format, the author presents the story of Ellis Island and the immigrants who passed through its doors. An electronic book.

Levine, Gail Carson. *Ella Enchanted.* New York: HarperCollins, 1997.
  In this novel based on the Cinderella tale, Ella proves to be a courageous and determined heroine.

Lewin, Ted. *I Was a Teenage Professional Wrestler.* New York: Orchard, 1993.
  An autobiography in which the author describes how he became a wrestler to earn money for art school.

Little, Jean. *Little by Little: A Writer's Education.* Markham, Ontario: Viking, 1987.
  A moving biography in which Little discusses the difficulties she encountered growing up as a legally blind child and her ultimate triumph.

Livingston, Myra Cohn, comp. *If You Ever Meet a Whale.* Illus. Leonard Everett Fisher. New York: Holiday House, 1992.
  A collection of poems about whales written by a variety of poets.

Locker, Thomas. *Water Dance.* San Diego: Harcourt Brace & Co., 1997.
  The author describes the various forms of water such as mist, seas, rivers, etc.

Mahy, Margaret. *My Mysterious World.* Photos David Alexander. Katonah, NY: Owen, 1995.
  New Zealand born Mahy discusses how she goes about writing her picture books and novels.

Martin, Rafe. *A Storyteller's Story.* Photos Jill Krementz. Katonah, NY: Owen, 1992.
  Martin describes his life in upstate New York for very young readers and shows how his storytelling and his writing are linked.

Matazzoni, Joe. *Robert Frost: Poems, Life, and Legacy.* Donald Sheehy, general ed. New York: Holt, 1998.
A CD-ROM that includes original documentary film on Frost's life, the complete texts of all his works, with Frost himself often the reader, critical essays, and much more.

Mayer, Mercer. *Just Grandma and Me.* Racine, WI: Western Publishing, 1983.
A young boy and his grandmother spend a day together at the beach. Available in English, Spanish, and Japanese. An electronic book.

———. *Little Monster at School.* New York: Green Frog, 1978.
Yally hates everything about school, but the kindness of his classmates finally wins him over. Available in English and Spanish. An electronic book.

McFarlane, Sheryl. *Waiting for the Whales.* Illus. Ron Lightburn. New York: Philomel, 1993.
A lonely old man who waits each year to see the orcas pass hopes to inspire his young granddaughter with his love of whales.

Microsoft Encarta '98 Encyclopedia Deluxe Edition. Redmond, WA: Microsoft, 1998.
Provides 32,000 articles and 10,000 Web site links.

Mitchell, Barbara. *Waterman's Child.* Illus. Daniel san Souci. New York: Lothrop, 1997.
Annie describes life in three generations of watermen's families on Chesapeake Bay.

My First Dictionary. New York: DK Publishing, 1996.
Defines and illustrates one thousand words commonly used by young children. An electronic book.

Myers, Walter Dean. *Harlem.* Illus. Christopher Myers. New York: Scholastic, 1997.
Myers traces the African American migration to the streets of Harlem, New York, in this poignant book.

———. *Malcolm X: By Any Means Necessary.* New York: Scholastic, 1993.
A biography of the civil rights leader for older readers. An electronic book.

Oppenheim, Shulamith Levey. *The Selchie's Seed.* Illus. Diane Goode. San Diego: Harcourt Brace, 1996.
A young girl who is descended from a line of seal folk becomes spellbound by a mysterious white whale.

Osborne, Mary Pope. *Favorite Greek Myths.* New York: Scholastic, 1993.
    An illustrated telling of twelve Greek myths. An electronic book.

Our Earth. Washington, DC: National Geographic, 1992.
    Four CD-ROM-based, picture-book stories about earth science, with simple maps.

Parker, Vic. *Bearobics.* Illus. Emily Bolan. New York: Viking, 1997.
    A counting book filled with wonderful pop-music action words.

Patent, Dorothy Hindshaw. *All About Whales.* New York: Holiday House, 1987.
    An introduction to the whale and its habits.

Paulsen, Gary. *The Car.* San Diego: Harcourt, 1994.
    A teen abandoned by his parents finds and assembles a kit car and takes to the open road.

_____. *The Crossing.* New York: Orchard, 1987.
    A ragged Mexican boy tries desperately to cross the border safely into the United States.

———. *Dancing Carl.* New York: Bradbury, 1983.
    Wearing a torn flight jacket, Carl expresses himself by frequently dancing on the ice rink.

_____. *Dogsong.* New York: Bradbury, 1985.
    A young Eskimo boy drives a dog sled 1400 miles across Alaska to discover the old ways of his people.

———. *Harris and Me: A Summer Remembered.* San Diego: Harcourt, 1993.
    Because his parents can't care for him properly, a young boy is sent to live on his relatives' farm. There he meets the indomitable Harris and embarks on a summer of crazy adventures. A tall, tall tale indeed!

_____. *Hatchet.* New York: Bradbury, 1987.
    When the small plane he is riding in crashes, thirteen-year-old Brian must survive in the Canadian woods with nothing but a hatchet. Here he comes to terms not only with nature, but also with his parents' divorce.

_____. *The Night the White Deer Died.* New York: Delacorte, 1990.
A teenage girl and an old Native American are brought together by the same haunting dream.

_____. *The Tortilla Factory.* Illus. Ruth Wright Paulsen. San Diego: Harcourt, 1995.
In lyrical prose, Paulsen describes the planting and harvesting of wheat and making of tortillas.

———. *The Winter Room.* New York: Orchard, 1989.
Written in lyrical prose which won Paulsen a Newbery Honor Award, this is the story of a young boy growing up on a Minnesota farm.

———. *Woodsong.* Illus. Ruth Wright Paulsen. New York: Bradbury, 1990.
Paulsen's account of his rugged life in the Minnesota woods, including his running of the famed Iditarod across Alaska.

_____. *Work Song.* Illus. Ruth Wright Paulsen. San Diego: Harcourt, 1997.
The author celebrates various kinds of work.

Peck, Richard. *Anonymously Yours.* Englewood Cliffs, NJ: Messner, 1991.
Peck started out as a teacher and eventually became a writer. In this book, he shows how his life and writing are connected.

Philip, Neil, sel. *Earth Always Endures.* Photos Edward S. Curtis. New York: Viking, 1996.
An anthology of sixty Native American poems accompanied by beautiful black and white photos.

Poe, Edgar Allan. "The Fall of the House of Usher." *"The Fall of the House of Usher" and Other Tales.* New York: New American Library, 1960. 113–31.
A young man marries his twin sister, which brings on a curse that leads to the ultimate destruction of his household. CD-ROM version available.

———. "The Tell-Tale Heart." *"The Tell-Tale Heart" and Other Writings by Edgar Allan Poe.* New York: Bantam, 1982. 1–9.
In this short story, the protagonist kills an old man, dismembers him, and buries him beneath his floor planks—only to be tortured by what he believes to be the ticking of the victim's heart. Available as an electronic book.

Polacco, Patricia. *Firetalking.* Photos. Lawrence Migdale. Katonah, NY: Owen, 1994.
The author writes about her Russian heritage and the inspiration for many of her children's books.

Pomerantz, Charlotte. *The Chalk Doll.* Illus. Frané Lessac. New York: HarperCollins, 1989.
A mother tells her daughter about a special doll and her childhood in Jamaica.

Prelutsky, Jack. *New Kid on the Block.* New York: Greenwillow, 1984.
Eighteen humorous poems selected from the larger volume of the same name in this electronic-book version.

Ray, Deborah Kogan. *My Daddy Was a Soldier: A World War II Story.* New York: Holiday House, 1990.
While her father is away fighting in the Pacific during World War II, a young girl works for the war effort at home.

Richter, Hans Peter. *I Was There.* Trans. Edite Kroll. New York: Viking, 1992.
A German boy tells of his experiences in the Hitler youth movement during the early years of the Third Reich.

Rosenberg, Liz. *Grandmother and the Runaway Shadow.* Illus. Beth Peck. San Diego: Harcourt, 1996.
A family story of a grandmother who escapes persecution of the Jews in eastern Europe and flees to America.

Rylant, Cynthia. *An Angel for Solomon Singer.* Illus. Peter Catalanotto. New York: Orchard, 1992.
Despite his lonely life in New York City, Solomon Singer keeps his dreams alive and finds companionship at the Westway Cafe.

_____. *Appalachia: The Voices of Sleeping Birds.* Illus. Barry Moser. San Diego: Harcourt, 1991.
In lyrical language, Rylant describes life in the Appalachian region.

_____. *Best Wishes.* Photos Carlo Ontal. Katonah, NY: Owen, 1992.
Very simple autobiography in which the author shows how her life and writing are connected.

_____. *But I'll Be Back Again: An Album.* New York: Orchard, 1988.
A frank autobiography for older children in which Rylant discusses her life and writing.

_____. *Children of Christmas: Stories for the Season.* New York: Orchard, 1987.
Short stories with Christmas themes.

_____. *Every Living Thing.* Illus. S. D. Schindler. New York: Bradbury, 1985.
Twelve short stories in which animals change people's lives for the better.

_____. *A Fine White Dust.* New York: Bradbury, 1986.
Thirteen-year-old Peter, stimulated by the arrival of a traveling preacher, tries to reconcile his religious beliefs with those of his family and friends.

_____. *Missing May.* New York: Orchard, 1992.
Summer and her uncle Ob try to come to grips with the death of May, Summer's dearly loved aunt.

_____. *When I Was Young in the Mountains.* New York: Dutton, 1982.
In hauntingly beautiful, repetitive language, Rylant describes her life with her grandparents in a coal mining town.

Say, Allen. *Grandfather's Journey.* Boston: Houghton, 1993.
A Japanese American man describes his grandfather's coming to America long ago and his grandparent's love of this country while at the same time longing for his homeland. Winner of the 1993 Caldecott Medal.

Schlichting, Mark. *Harry and the Haunted House.* Los Angeles: Random House/Broderbund, 1994.
When one of them hits a ball through the window of a house they believe to be haunted, five friends work up their courage to go in and get it. Available in English and Spanish. An electronic book.

———, retell. *The Tortoise and the Hare.* Los Angeles: Random House/Broderbund, 1993.
A slow tortoise, by his persistence, beats a boastful rabbit in a race. Available in English and Spanish. An electronic book.

Simon, Seymour. *The Brain: Our Nervous System.* New York: Morrow, 1997.
A clear discussion of the workings of the brain and nervous system, accompanied by marvelous photographs.

_____. *The Heart: Our Circulatory System.* New York: Morrow, 1996.
This book describes the workings of the heart and circulatory system, and includes marvelous photographs.

Soto, Gary. *Canto Familiar.* Illus. Annika Nelson. San Diego: Harcourt, 1995.
A collection of poems about familiar moments in the lives of Mexican Americans.

_____. *In Chato's Kitchen.* Illus. Susan Guevara. New York: Putnam, 1995.
Two cats prepare a welcome party for their new neighbors, a family of mice, intending to serve the mice as the main course.

Sperry, Armstrong. *Call it Courage.* New York: Simon & Schuster, 1983.
A young boy overcomes his fear of the sea and proves to himself and his tribe that he is courageous.

Stanley, Diane. *Saving Sweetness.* Illus. G. Brian Karas. New York: Putnam, 1996.
A sheriff sets out to rescue an orphan named Sweetness from the nasty Mrs. Sump, unaware of the child's unusual resourcefulness.

Stevenson, James. *Don't You Know There's a War On.* New York: Greenwillow, 1992.
Stevenson writes about his various childhood activities during World War II: collecting newspapers and scrap metal, planting a victory garden, and so forth. He makes it clear that those at home faced deprivations, too.

———. *July.* New York: Greenwillow, 1990.
Stevenson recalls the summers he and his brother spent at the shore with their grandparents.

———. *The Pattaconk Brook.* New York: Greenwillow, 1993.
Sidney the Frog writes down in his notebook the sounds he hears at the brook and is joined by Sherry the Snail. Wonderful when introducing writing notebooks.

———. *Sweet Corn.* New York: Greenwillow, 1995.
A collection of short poems filled with delightful imagery.

Taylor, Theodore. *The Hostage.* New York: Delacorte, 1987.
A young boy grapples with whether a killer whale should be captured and sold to an amusement park to provide his family with much-needed money or allowed to remain free.

Tom Snyder Productions. *Fizz & Martina in Tough Krudd.* Watertown, MA, 1992.
Krudd, a bully, makes life miserable for Fizz until a scary adventure forces Krudd to rethink his nasty attitude. An electronic book.

_____. *Flodd the Bad Guy.* Watertown, MA, 1994.
Students decide how to help Alex use three wishes from his magic lamp to soften Flodd's mean-spirited heart. An electronic book.

_____. *Hansel and Gretel.* Watertown, MA, 1993.
In this modern twist on a classic tale, Hansel and Gretel wander into the Endless Forest because their parents are busy watching television. Instead of discovering a gingerbread house, they come upon a house made of television sets! An electronic book.

_____. *Hilary and the Beast.* Watertown, MA, 1993.
Readers follow Hilary, a brave and smart seven-year-old, on her adventures as she rescues and befriends a lovable beast from a traveling circus. An electronic book.

_____. *Jack and the Beanstalk.* Watertown, MA, 1993.
Should Jack go all the way to the top of the beanstalk or climb off and explore the inside of a cloud? Readers of this electronic book get to decide.

Twain, Mark. *The Adventures of Tom Sawyer.* New York: Southern Star Interactive, 1996.
A CD-ROM that includes the compete text of the novel, a biography of the author, and a narrated slide show.

Twain, Mark. *Twain's World.* Parsippany, NJ: Bureau Development, 1993.
The complete works of Mark Twain on CD-ROM, enhanced with pictures and animation.

Uchida, Yoshiko. *The Invisible Thread: An Autobiography.* Englewood Cliffs, NJ: Messner, 1991.
Uchida, a Japanese American, describes growing up in Berkeley, California and her family's internment in a concentration camp during World War II.

Vogel, Ilse Margaret. *Bad Times, Good Friends: A Personal Memoir.* San Diego: Harcourt, 1992.

Vogel describes how she and some of her friends survived Nazi domination in Berlin from 1943 to 1945.

Weller, Frances Ward. *I Wonder If I'll See a Whale.* Illus. Ted Lewin. New York: Philomel, 1991.

A youngster observes a humpback whale from a whale watching boat. Includes factual information on whales spotted off the northeast coast of the United States.

Wells, Rosemary. *Bunny Cakes.* New York: Dial, 1997.

Young Max tries repeatedly to write a note the grocer can understand so he can get Red-Hot Marshmallow Squirters to decorate the earthworm cake he is making for his grandmother's birthday.

White, E. B. *The Trumpet of the Swan.* Illus. Edward Frascino. New York: Harper, 1979.

Even though he is a mute swan, Lewis learns to play the trumpet and write and successfully wins the swan of his dreams.

Wiesel, Elie. *Night.* New York: Bantam, 1982.

The author's account of the horrors he suffered in a Nazi concentration camp.

A World of Animals. Washington, DC: National Geographic, 1992.

Five CD-ROM-based, picture-book stories about "Butterflies," "Dinosaurs," "Farm Animals," "Spiders," and "Whales." The books discuss physical characteristics, habitats, food, reproduction, and life cycles.

A World of Plants. Washington, DC: National Geographic, 1993.

Four CD-ROM-based picture books about plants: "The Parts of a Plant"; "What Is a Seed?"; "A Tree Through the Seasons"; and "Plants Are Important."

Yep, Laurence. *The Lost Garden.* Englewood Cliffs, NJ: Messner, 1991.

The author describes his life as a Chinese American growing up in San Francisco, California, and how he celebrates his ethnic heritage in his writing.

Yolen, Jane. *A Letter from Phoenix Farm.* Photos Jason Stemple. Katonah, NY: Owen, 1992.

In this simple autobiography, Yolen shows young readers how she performs the dual role of writer and editor.

Professional Literature

Byrum, Donna, and Virginia Lazenby Pierce. "Bringing Children to Literacy Through Theme Cycles." *Bringing Children to Literacy: Classrooms at Work.* Ed. Bill Harp. Norwood, MA: Christopher-Gordon, 1993.

Calkins, Lucy McCormick. *Living Between the Lines.* Portsmouth, NH: Heinemann, 1991.
The author discusses various facets of teaching writing and the use of writers' notebooks.

Children's Books in Print. New Providence, NJ: Bowker, updated annually.
Continuously updated, this excellent reference work lists all the children's books currently in print, giving title, author, illustrator, publisher, copyright date, price, suggested ages, ISBN number, and whether a paper edition has been printed. There are three volumes: author, title, illustrator. Also contains an extensive list of publishers' names and addresses.

Gallo, Donald R., ed. *Author's Insights: Turning Teenagers into Readers and Writers.* Portsmouth, NH: Heinemann, 1992.
Twelve chapters, each written by a prominent author for young adults. Filled with insights about the author's lives and writings.

Harp, Bill, ed. *Bringing Children to Literacy: Classrooms at Work.* Norwood, MA: Christopher-Gordon, 1993.
Ten practicing teachers of different grade levels contribute chapters on the teaching of reading and writing.

Harwayne, Shelley. *Lasting Impressions: Weaving Literature into the Writing Workshop.* Portsmouth, NH: Heinemann, 1992.
In this practical book, Harwayne demonstrates how to create lifelong readers and writers. She shows how to use literature to help students find writing topics to use in conferences, to teach listening skills, and much more. A treasure.

Huck, Charlotte S., Susan Hepler, Janet Hickman, and Barbara Z. Kiefer. *Children's Literature in the Elementary School.* 6th ed. Dubuque, IA: McGraw-Hill, 1997.
A comprehensive text on the history of children's literature, the different genres, criteria for selection, and ideas for using literature in the classroom.

Lobel, Arnold. "Show Me the Way to Go Home." *The Horn Book* 65 (1989): 29.
> The author talks about his life and why he writes for children.

Peterson, Ralph. *Life in a Crowded Place: Making a Learning Community.* Portsmouth, NH: Heinemann, 1992.
> Peterson shows how teachers can work with their students to create a classroom community.

Peterson, Ralph, and Maryann Eeds, eds. *Grand Conversations: Literature Groups in Action.* New York: Scholastic, 1990.
> This brief eighty-page book gives suggestions for developing students' awareness of literary elements such as story structure, plot, characters. Invaluable!

Rosenblatt, Louise. *The Reader, the Text, the Poem.* Carbondale, IL: Southern Illinois Press, 1978.
> Rosenblatt discusses the central role of the reader and the reader's response in making meaning from text. This book, along with her *Literature As Exploration,* has become a classic reference for reader response theory.

Routman, Regie. *Invitations: Changing as Teachers and Learners K–12.* Portsmouth, NH: Heinemann, 1991.
> This big book (over five-hundred pages) offers a wealth of practical information for teachers who have already moved into whole language teaching. Routman calls on her experience working with teachers throughout the grades to offer practical suggestions for teaching reading and writing, using literature, working with at-risk students, and more.

Shanahan, Timothy, ed. *Reading and Writing Together: New Perspectives for the Classroom.* Norwood, MA: Christopher-Gordon, 1990.
> Eleven chapters, each written by a thoughtful classroom teacher on the theory and practice of teaching reading and writing. Practical ideas with a sound theoretical basis.

Something About the Author. Autobiography Series. Detroit, MI: Gale Research Co., 1986–.
> A set of encyclopedic books containing biographical information on children's book authors.

Wolf, Shelby Ann, and Shirley Brice Heath. "The Net of Story." *The Horn Book* 69 (1993): 705.
> The authors write about the influence of story in children's lives.

Yolen, Jane. *Touch Magic.* New York: Philomel, 1991.
> Yolen, a prolific writer of fantasy herself, speaks about writing this genre and its impact on lives.

Additional Resources

Reading and Writing

American Library Association (ALA), 50 East Huron Street, Chicago, IL 60611.
> Publishes *Booklist.*

Baker and Taylor Book Company, 50 Kirby Avenue, Sommerville, NJ 08876-0734.
> Offers book discounts of as much as 40 percent.

Book Links, 434 W. Downer, Aurora, IL 60506.

Bulletin of the Center for Children's Books, University of Illinois Press, 54 E. Gregory Drive, Champaign, IL 61820.

Children's Book Council, 568 Broadway, Suite 404, New York, NY 10012-0706.

The Horn Book, 14 Beacon Street, Boston, MA 02108.

Ingram Library Services, Inc. 1125 Heil Quaker Blvd., LaVergne, TN 37086-1986.
> Offers book discounts of as much as 43 percent.

International Reading Association (IRA), 800 Barksdale Road, PO Box 8139, Newark, DE 19714-8139.
> Publishes *The Reading Teacher.*

Modern Language Association. 10 Astor Place, New York, NY 10003-6981.

New Advocate, 480 Washington Street, Norwood, MA 02108.

National Council of Teachers of English. 1111 W. Kenyon Road, Urbana, IL 61801-1096.
Publishes *English Journal* and *Language Arts;* sponsors the Assembly on Literature for Adolescents publication, *ALAN Review,* and the NCTENet online discussion area.

Scholastic, Inc., P.O. Box 7502, 2931 East McCarty Street, Jefferson City, MO 65102.
Publishes *Electronic Learning* and *Instructor* magazines. Offers Scholastic Book Club and Scholastic Network, a nationwide online service created especially for educators.

School Library Journal, 249 W. 17th Street, New York, NY 10011.

Teaching K–8, 40 Richards Avenue, Norwalk, CT 06854.

Troll Book Club, 100 Corporate Drive, Mahwah, NJ 07430.

Trumpet Book Club, 666 Fifth Avenue, 35th floor, New York, NY 10103 (Bantam, Doubleday, Dell).

Voice of Youth Advocates (VOYA), Scarecrow Press, Dept. VOYA, 52 Liberty Street, P.O. Box 4167, Metuchen, NJ 08840.

Computers

ACE Journal: The Journal of the NCTE Assembly on Computers in English, National Council of Teachers of English, 1111 W. Kenyon Road, Urbana, IL 61801-1096.

Armstrong, Sara. *Telecommunications in the Classroom.* Eugene, OR: Computer Learning Foundation and International Society for Technology in Education, 1995.

Association for Educational Communications and Technology (AECT), 1025 Vermont Avenue, NW, Suite 820, Washington, DC 20005-3547.

Association for Supervision and Curriculum Development, 1250 N. Pitt Street, Alexandria, VA 22314-1453.
Publishes *Curriculum/Technology Quarterly.*

Bailey, Gerald, and Gwen Bailey. *101 Activities for Creating Effective Technology Staff Development Programs.* New York: Scholastic, 1993.

Bailey, Gerald, and Dan Lumley. *Creating a Technology Staff Development Program: An Administrator's Sourcebook for Redefining Teaching and Learning.* New York: Scholastic, 1993.

Balliot, Robert L., and David P. Habib. "How to Search the World Wide Web: A Tutorial and Guide for Beginners." **http://www.ultranet.com/~egrlib/tutor.htm.**

BookWorm (716) 544-2439.
    Publishes computer software.

Broderbund Software, Inc., 500 Redwood Blvd., P.O. Box 6121, Novato, CA 94948-6121.

Bureau Development Inc., 141 New Road, Parsippany, NJ 07054, (201) 808-2700.
    Publishes computer software.

"CASO's Internet University: Your Guide to Online College Courses." **http://caso.com/.**

Cetron, Marvin, and Margaret Gayle. *Educational Renaissance: Our Schools at the Turn of the Century.* New York: St. Martin's Press, 1991.

Computer Curriculum Corporation, 1287 Lawrence Station Road, Sunnyvale, CA 94089, (800) 455-7910.

Computerized Educational Resources, 1313 5th Street SE, Minneapolis, MN 55414.
    Publishes computer software.

Computers and Composition: An International Journal for Teachers of Writing. Ablex Publishing Corp., 355 Chestnut St., Norwood, NJ 07648.

Cotton, Eileen Giuffré. *The Online Classroom: Teaching with the Internet.* 2nd ed. ERIC Clearinghouse, 1997.

Davidson and Associates, 19840 Pioneer Avenue, Torrance, CA 90503-1660, (800) 545-7677.

Derfler, Frank. J., and Les Freed. *How Networks Work.* Emeryville, CA: Davis Press, 1996.

Dern, Daniel P. *The Internet Guide for New Users.* New York: McGraw-Hill, 1994.

Discis Knowledge Research, 41 Sheppard Avenue, Suite 410, Toronto, Ontario M2N5W9.

DK Publishing, Inc. 95 Madison Avenue, New York, NY 10016. **http://www.dk.com.** In addition to children's books, this company produces fine computer software.

Dockterman, Dr. David. *Great Teaching in the One Compuer Classroom.* 5th ed. Watertown, MA: Tom Snyder Productions, 1998.
Dockterman offers practical solutions for using a single computer to spark discussion and learning.

Educational Support Systems, 1505 Black Mountain Road, Hillsborough, CA 94010.
Produces computer software.

Educator's Internet Funding Guide: Classroom Connect's Reference Guide to Technology Funding. Lancaster, PA: Wentworth Worldwide Media, 1996.

Educators' Tech Exchange, P.O. Box 52180, Pacific Grove, CA 93950.

Electronic Learning, Scholastic, Inc., PO Box 7502, 2931 East McCarty Street, Jefferson City, MO 65102.

Ellsworth, Jill H. *Education on the Internet.* Indianapolis: Sams, 1994.

Facts on File, Inc., 11 Penn Plaza, New York, NY 10001, (800) 322-8755.
Produces computer software.

First Adventures Bookshelf. Sunnyvale, CA: Computer Curriulum Corporation, 1994.
Twenty-two electronic books are available, sixteen in English and six in Spanish, for children in grades 1 and 2. These books provide interactive opportunities that support reading, writing, listening, and speaking.

Fraase, Michael. *The PC Internet Tour.* Chapel Hill, NC: Ventana Press, 1994.

Franklin Electronic Publishers Burlington, NJ. **http://www.franklin.com.**

Grolier Electronic Publishing, Inc., Sherman Turnpike, Danbury, CT 06816, (203) 797-3530.

Hahn, H., and R. Stout. *The Internet Yellow Pages.* Berkeley, CA: Osborne McGraw-Hill, 1996.

HarperCollins, 10 East 53rd Street, New York, NY 10022, (800) 424-6234.
In addition to its line of children's books, Harper has produced some computer software.

Hartley, a division of Jostens Learning Corporation, 9920 Pacific Heights Blvd., San Diego, CA 92121, (800) 521-8538.
Produces computer software.

Heide, Ann, and Linda Stilborne. *The Teacher's Complete and Easy Guide to the Internet.* Newark, DE: International Reading Association (IRA), 1996.

Henry Holt, 115 West 18th Street, New York, NY 10011, (212) 886-9200.
Source of CD-ROM on Robert Frost.

Institute for Academic Technology, 2525 Meridian Parkway, Suite 400, Durham, NC 27713.

Institute for Research and Learning, 2550 Hanover Street, Palo Alto, CA 94304-1115.

International Society for Technology in Education (ISTE), University of Oregon, 1787 Agate Street, Eugene, OR 97403-9905.
Publishes the newsletter *ISTE Update;* the journals *Learning and Leading with Technology* and the *Journal of Computing in Teacher Education;* and Proceedings from the NECC conferences.

Internet World, Mecklermedia Corp., 20 Ketchum St., Westport, CT 06880.

Kehoe, Brendan P. *Zen and the Art of the Internet: A Beginner's Guide.* Englewood
 Cliffs, NJ: Prentice-Hall, 1996.

Language Arts WebGuide. Lancaster, PA: Classroom Connect, Wentworth Worldwide
 Media, 1997.

Leu, Donald J., Deborah Diadium Leu, and Katherine R. Leu, *Teaching with the Internet:
 Lessons from the Classroom.* Norwood, MA: Christopher-Gordon, 1997.
 Provides clear instructions and numerous teaching suggestions for teaching with
 the Internet.

Marks, Tracy. "Windweaver's Search Guide."
 http://www.windweaver.com/searchguide.htm.

McClain, Tim, and Chris Sturm. *Net-Seminar.* Torrance, CA: Classroom Connect,
 1998.
 A do-it-yourself kit for technology trainers that provides information for con
 ducting successful seminars.

Microsoft Corporation, Redmond, WA, 1-800-426-9400.

Milliken Publishing Company, 1100 Research Blvd. P.O. Box 21579, St. Louis, MO
 63132, (800) 325-4136.
 Source for computer software.

Monroe, Rick. *Writing and Thinking with Computers: A Practical and Progressive Approach.* Urbana, IL: NCTE, 1993.

Morris, Evan. *The Booklover's Guide to the Internet.* New York: Fawcett Columbine,
 1996.

Moursund, David. *Obtaining Resources for Technology in Education: A How to Guide
 for Writing Proposals, Forming Partnerships, and Raising Funds.* Eugene, OR:
 International Society for Technology in Education (ISTE), 1996
 Office of Technology Assessment, U.S. Congress. Order reports from: U.S. Government Printing Office, Washington, DC 20402.

Only the Best: The Annual Guide to Highest-Rated Education Software/Multimedia for Preschool–Grade 12. Association for Supervision and Curriculum Development (ASCD), Technology Resource Center, 1250 N. Pitt Street, Alexandria, VA 22314.

Queue, 338 Commerce Drive, Fairfield, CT 06430. Computer software.

Rodrigues, Dawn. *The Research Paper and the World Wide Web.* Upper Saddle River, NJ: Prentice-Hall, 1997.

Roerdon, Laura Parker. *Net Lessons: Web-Based Projects for Your Classroom,* Sebastopol, CA: O'Reilly, 1997.
Provides more than one hundred classroom-tested Internet lesson plans and ideas for K–12.

Sharp, Vicki. *Computer Education for Teachers,* 2nd ed. Eugene, OR: International Society for Technology in Education (ISTE), 1996.

Shumate, Michael. "Tracing the Growth of a New Literature." **http://www.december. com/cmc/mag/1996/dec/shumate.html**.

Southern Star Interactive, 57 East 11th Street, New York, NY 10211. Produces computer software.

Sperling, Dave. *The Internet Guide For English Language Teachers.* Upper Saddle River, NJ: Prentice-Hall, 1997.

Sullivan, Patricia, and Jennie Dautermann, eds. *Electronic Literacies in the Workplace: Technologies of Writing.* Urbana, IL: National Council of Teachers of English (NCTE), 1996.

Teaching Language Arts with the Internet, Lancaster, PA: Classroom Connect, Wentworth Worldwide Media, 1997.

Technology and Learning, Peter Li, Inc., P.O. Box 49727, Dayton OH 45449-0727.

T.H.E. (Technological Horizons in Education) Journal, 150 El Camino Real, Suite 112, Tustin, CA 92780-3670.

Tom Snyder Productions, 80 Coolidge Hill Road, Watertown, MA 02172 2817. (800) 342-0236. Computer software.

Westwind Media, Box 27578, Panama City, FL 32411. (904) 235-3579.

Wresch, William, ed. *The English Classroom in the Computer Age: Thirty Lesson Plans.* Urbana, IL: NCTE, 1991.

Authors

Marilyn Jody, Ph.D., has taught English and American literature at the university level for more than thirty years. She currently holds the rank of professor emeritus at Western Carolina University, where she has been head of the English department and director of the WCU MicroNet BookRead Project. As visiting professor of English education at Teachers College, Columbia University, she helped establish and was co-coordinator of the Teachers College Literature Project. She has been a visiting scholar in American literature at Yunnan University and at the Beijing Institute of Technology in the People's Republic of China, and has held teaching positions at the University of Alaska, the University of Dayton, the University of North Carolina at Charlotte, and Indiana University. At present she is living in the mountains of North Carolina, teaching, writing her next book, and consulting on the use of computers in the English classroom.

Marianne Saccardi, M.A., taught in public and private elementary schools for twenty years and is currently teaching children's literature and writing at Norwalk Community-Technical College, in Connecticut, and the College of New Rochelle, in New York. She is also a consultant for Broderbund Software, writing bibliographies and themes for use with the company's electronic books, and a children's book reviewer for *School Library Journal.* She founded the Fairfield-Westchester Children's Reading Project, which supplied thousands of books over five years to schoolchildren in New York and Connecticut. With Marilyn Jody, she founded BookRead, a national electronic-mail system linking children, authors, and books. She has conducted numerous workshops on children's literature and writing in Connecticut and New York and has presented workshops at the conventions of the International Reading Association and the National Council of Teachers of English. Her articles have appeared in *School Library Journal, The Reading Teacher, School Arts,* and *The Constructive Triangle.* Her book, *Art in Story: Teaching Art to Elementary School Children,* was published by the Shoe String Press/Linner Professional Publications in 1997.

Contributors

Sue Ellen Bridgers's first novel, *Home Before Dark,* was published in 1976, to high critical acclaim. Her subsequent books have won many awards. To name just a few of them, *All Together Now* (1978), received the Christopher Award, was the winner of the Boston Globe-Horn Book Award for Fiction, and was an ALA Notable Children's Book as well as a Best Book for Young Adults. *Home Before Dark* (1976), *Notes for Another Life* (1981), *Sarah Will* (1985), and *Permanent Connections* (1987) are all ALA Best Books for Young Adults. In 1985, Ms. Bridgers received the ALAN Award from the Assembly on Literature for Adolescents of the National Council of Teachers of English for her outstanding contributions to young adult literature.

Born in Washington, D.C. and raised in a family of naturalists, **Jean Craighead George**'s life centered around writing and nature. She attended Pennsylvania State University, graduating with degrees in English and science. In the 1940s, she was a member of the White House press corps and a reporter for *The Washington Post.* Ms. George, who has written over sixty books—among them *My Side of the Mountain,* a 1960 Newbery Honor Book, and its 1990 sequel *On the Far Side of the Mountain*—also hikes, canoes, and makes sourdough pancakes. In 1991, Ms. George became the first winner of the School Library Media Section of the New York Library Association's Knickerbocker Award for Juvenile Literature, which was presented to her for the "consistent superior quality" of her literary works.

Howard Holden graduated from Guilford College in 1984 with a major in English. He spent five years as a whitewater raft guide on rivers in the Southeastern United States. Following an auto accident that ended his whitewater career, he studied journalism and English as a graduate student at Western Carolina University, then moved on to an internship at CNN in Atlanta. He is currently a freelance writer and a reporter for a small newspaper in Roswell, Georgia.

John Scott Kemp is currently completing his thesis for the master's degree in English at Western Carolina University, while he teaches both English and microcomputer systems at two community colleges in North Carolina. He has won numerous academic honors as well as awards for scholarly articles and expects publication in December 1995 of his essay "'Say First'

AAO-5990

Earthly Muse: Miltonic Influence in Pope's 'Essay on Man.'" He was named "Outstanding Graduate in Business Computer Science" at Tri-County Community College and also awarded the scholarship for "Highest Distinction in English" at Western Carolina University.

Gary Paulsen is a versatile and prolific writer whose life of adventure has found its way into more than forty books and two hundred articles. It is Paulsen's books for young people that have brought him the most professional recognition. His awards began in 1976 with the Central Missouri Award for Children's Literature and have continued almost yearly since. *The Green Recruit* was named to the *New York Times* list of Best Books for Young Adults in 1980, and *Sailing from Jibs to Jibbing* followed in 1982. The American Library Association included *Dancing Carl* on its Best Young Adult Books list in 1983, and *Tracker* made the list in 1984, as well as receiving the 1985 Society of Midland Authors award for young adult literature. The prestigious Newbery Honor Book award went to *Dogsong* in 1986, to *Hatchet* in 1988, and to *The Winter Room* in 1990.

Randy Pitts, who recently completed his master's degree in English at Western Carolina University, is a computer specialist and published poet. He writes: "I remember buying an ATARI 2600 in 1981 because I was tired of shoveling quarters in video games. Being limited to games was boring, so I bought a Commodore 64. I was hooked: games . . . word processing, word processing . . . games. What else was there to life? I moved up to an Amiga 1000, then a 1200, then added an IBM 386, then a 486. At work (in the computer field, 1985) I had an Apple II+. In graduate school, studying English, I tackled the various incarnations of Macintoshes. . . . End Result? I think computers are great as tools, but they should never replace teachers."